D1453372

# CACTUS IDENTIFIER

## including succulent plants

By

**HELMUT BECHTEL**

*With photographs*
*by the author*

**STERLING PUBLISHING CO., INC.** NEW YORK

*Oak Tree Press Co., Ltd.*

## OTHER BOOKS OF INTEREST

Cage Bird Identifier
Colorful Mineral Identifier
Herb Identifier & Handbook
House Plant Identifier

Marine Aquarium Fish Identifier
Seashell Collectors' Handbook &
  Identifier
Tropical Fish Identifier

Adapted from the German book, "Bunte Welt der Kakteen,"
© 1975 by Franckh'sche Verlagshandlung, W. Keller & Co.,
Stuttgart, West Germany. Translated by Manly Banister.
Adapted by E. W. Egan.

Photographs by the author

Published 1977 by Sterling Publishing Co., Inc.
419 Park Avenue South, New York, N.Y. 10016
Distributed in Australia and New Zealand by Oak Tree Press Co., Ltd.,
P.O. Box J34, Brickfield Hill, Sydney 2000, N.S.W.
Distributed in the United Kingdom and elsewhere in the British Commonwealth
by Ward Lock Ltd., 116 Baker Street, London W 1
Printed in Hong Kong
Library of Congress Catalog Card No.: 76-51168
Sterling ISBN 0-8069-3080-2 Trade     Oak Tree 7061-2537-1
3081-0 Library

# Contents

# Introduction

All succulent plants, whether cacti or species from other families, have in common their adaptation to extremely dry climatic zones. The conditions of their native climate must be reproduced in cultivation. Because of their low humidity requirement, many of these hardy plants get along better in the dry air of our centrally heated dwellings than do other house plants. The unusual shapes of the cacti and other succulents are reason enough for cultivating them. In addition, many of them, especially cacti, produce lovely blossoms which rival other house-plant flowers in beauty. It is no wonder, then, that cacti—and other succulents in lesser measure—are constantly adding to their long list of friends. Many of the most beautiful cacti, such as *Lobivia, Rebutia, Parodia,* and many others, are especially easy for beginners to grow. It goes without saying that there are sensitive species which belong in a greenhouse, because they grow poorly in the house and fail to bloom. Most of the species discussed in this book, however, place no unusual demands on us. Cacti are available on the market in large numbers as both plants and seeds. Other succulents, in spite of being equally beautiful, are offered today in much smaller quantity, so that it is not always easy to obtain the desired species.

## CARE OF SUCCULENT PLANTS

If we wish to cultivate cactus and other succulents successfully, we must offer them living conditions which approximate most closely those of their original habitat. Only well-cared-for plants will show off their full beauty. For this reason, we should know what climatic and ecological conditions they are accustomed to and how they have adapted themselves to their often unfriendly surroundings.

The climate of the regions from which these plants come is characterized by lengthy dry periods and light rainfall. Nightly dew or formation of fog near the coast in certain regions provides some moisture in addition to the occasional rain. The abrupt transition between the dry and rainy seasons determines the yearly life-rhythm of succulents, all of which go through pronounced rest and growth periods. Add to this the great drop in temperature between day and night for which the hot, dry zones of our Earth are noted. Plants from high mountain regions, such as cacti of the Andes, experience this same contrast in temperature. In spite of low night temperatures, which can drop below 0° C. (32° F.), the sun in the daytime, at least locally, causes the air and soil to become very warm. The range of New World cacti, for example, extends from the United States to the southern tip of South America and from the coastal regions to an altitude of 3,000 and 4,000 metres

(9,842 and 13,123 feet). All these cacti are subject to the strong contrast of growth and rest seasons as well as the drop between day- and night-time temperatures.

Among succulents of the Old World, the circumstances are no different. The epiphytic cacti of the wet forests of South and Central America, such as *Rhipsalis, Epiphyllum, Nopalxochia* and so forth, constitute exceptions. These species do not undergo a pronounced dry season, but, in spite of this, they do need a rest period for the development of blossoms. They are cultivated in a manner similar to other epiphytic, flowering house plants.

Succulent plants must be kept where they can survive the long dry periods without damage. They store up water in the fleshy tissues of stems, branches, leaves and roots. A thick outer skin covering leaves that are reduced to mere spines—the designation thorn is incorrect—and the smallest possible surface area (provided by a spherical shape, for example) are factors that minimize evaporation from these plants in blazing sunshine. Not all of them, however, favor full sunlight, but many small species grow in semi-shade under rocks, boulders or bushes. Succulent plants possessing normal leaves cast them off during the rest season. Others, among them many cacti and mesembryanthemums (fig-marigolds or ice plants) withdraw into the ground. All of them require only temporary measures to be taken against the dry season, because at this time the succulents stop their growth.

The spines protect the plants from being eaten by animals—a serious problem in sterile regions where every green thing is welcome nourishment. Defenceless species protect themselves by means of poisonous sap or by camouflage which lets them blend into their surroundings.

In the brief span of this introduction, it is impossible to describe in detail all the measures of cultivation. Hints and tips amounting to catch-words must therefore suffice. Demands of cultivation that deviate from the rule in respect to individual species will be dealt with in the descriptive text accompanying the illustrations.

## LOCATION IN SUMMER AND IN WINTERING OVER

Indispensable to the welfare of all succulents is the severe change from rest to growth. Where no greenhouse is available, the cactus grower must, as a rule, locate his plants in different places in summer and winter. In the growth period, most species like to be where it is bright, sunny, warm and airy. Where a garden or patio is at one's disposal, it is best to keep the plants in the warm period of the year in the open, where they will receive more air and light than when placed in a window. Moreover, the important nightly cooling-off has a stronger effect in the open. During the rest period, the temperature as a rule should range from 5 to 12° C. (41 to 53° F.). Although succulent plants in their original habitat do not experience the change from warm to cold seasons that we do, when they are among us, they adapt themselves to this rhythm if we keep them cool and dry during the light-poor season. Not all plants will adapt themselves in this manner. Some fig-marigolds will bloom, of all times, in our winter.

## LIGHT AND WARMTH

Most succulent plants require a lot of light and warmth. Many species, however (for example, many Haworthias), grow in half-shade. Also, warmth-loving, light-hungry plants do not tolerate excessive amounts of glaring sunlight and will burn in these circumstances. If they are kept under glass, care must be taken to provide them with plenty of air in sunny weather to keep the heat-level from building up too high in the container. After wintering over, the plants should not be set out in the full sun without first undergoing a period of transition.

## PLANT CONTAINERS

You have a choice between water-permeable clay pots and water-tight, plastic containers. Both have advantages and disadvantages. If you place succulents singly on a window sill, plastic containers may be used to keep the soil from drying out too quickly. If single pots are placed together in a container or flat filled with peat, clay pots are preferred. These not only give off moisture but also take it up from the surrounding peat layer, which is kept slightly damp, so that the pots do not completely dry out. Pots of this kind brought together in a flat container filled with peat moss can be set out in the place most favorable for them, depending on the season, without trouble. If the flat or container is provided with a glass cover, it can be left out in the open even in rainy weather. In this way living conditions are obtained similar to those in a hot bed. A free flow of air must be maintained at all times. Flat-rooted and clump-building plants, such as Stapelia and Lithops relatives, develop well in flats.

## SOIL

Potting mix for succulent plants should be especially loose and porous, so that in watering the moisture will be well taken up and no wet puddles will form. It should be lime-free (except for certain hairy cacti) and of ample quantity, but should not contain nutritive materials that are too rich. It should be mixed up out of rotted leaf mold, coarse sand, garden soil and friable loam, and perlite or pumice-gravel. Special, ready-mixed soils for cacti, fig-marigolds and other succulents are available on the market.

## WATERING

During the growing season, succulent plants require a great deal of water and, on top of that, additional moisture is needed, to be stored within the plant for use during the dry season. In their original habitat, succulents usually undergo brief but heavy rainfall. Thus, when they are watered, they should be watered heavily. However, hold off the next watering until the first one has been fully absorbed and the soil feels dry not only on the surface but at a depth of an inch or so. In no circumstances should you begin watering too early at the end of the rest period. When in doubt, it is better to water too little than too much. In every case, standing water causes damage. For this reason, take care to lay a piece of broken clay pot or some gravel in the bottom of the pot to keep the drain hole open and prevent its plugging up.

Soft, lime-poor rainwater is best for your purposes—as a rule, tap water from the household pipes must be treated before using it on your plants, by adding a water-softener, obtainable from your local dealers. When watering, occasionally add a small amount of regular commercial, nitrogen-poor cactus fertilizer. However, avoid adding too much nourishment, which would only damage the plants.

The instructions on the label should tell you the proper amount. If not, ask your dealer. It goes without saying that the plants are to be fertilized only during the growing season.

## REPOTTING

As a general principle, succulents should be transplanted when the pots they are growing in actually become too small. Succulents, however, flower more freely and do better in pots that are not too big. In general, for barrel-shaped, globose or columnar plants, the pot should be about an inch or two wider than the plant itself. Do not water immediately after repotting, but wait a day or two. In this way, if the roots were damaged during transplanting they will have a chance to heal. Subjecting broken or bruised roots to water can cause rot. New clay pots should be soaked in water before being put to use. Group- or cushion-forming plants should not be divided, for they then lose much of their beauty.

## PROPAGATION

Many cacti and other succulents are especially easy to propagate by means of cuttings or by layering. Before planting the cutting that has been cut off with a clean, sharp knife, let the cut surface dry out. This can take longer than a week. Afterwards, place the cuttings erect in sand, peat, or some similar, highly porous material, so that the roots will really strike downward. It is especially easy when working with species whose offspring send out roots while they are still attached to the mother plant, or which produce already rooted offsets.

Propagation by means of seeds, which can be bought commercially at a reasonable price, requires extreme cleanliness, since the tender seedlings are especially susceptible to diseases, especially, propagation fungus. The seeds should be placed in loose substratum soil and sprout best at temperatures between 25 to 30° C. (77 to 86° F.). Night temperatures should be somewhat lower. In grafting, delicate, poorly-growing species are joined to a sturdier stock. Plants lacking chlorophyll, which therefore cannot exist independently, have to be grafted in order to live. Poorly-growing species thrive better grafted onto a good stock, and even root-diseased specimens can, circumstances permitting, be saved. We should, however, restrict grafting except on unavoidable occasions, as grafted plants are not as attractive to the eye and can, through excessive growth, acquire a form and appearance not characteristic of their species.

## DISEASES

Healthy, unpampered plants are the least prone to diseases and pests. For this reason, good care is the best prevention. If we observe the plants attentively, we can treat them at the right time. Among the most feared diseases are fungus attacks caused by wet- and dry-rot. Attacked areas must be removed immediately. Since rot, as a rule, begins in the roots, the still healthy part of the plant can sometimes be saved by grafting. It goes without saying that extreme cleanliness must be maintained in grafting. Often there is no choice but to destroy the plant. For protection against animal pests, highly effective chemical plant sprays are available. These must be kept out of reach of children and should be applied out-of-doors and not in the house. Among the most stubborn pests is the tiny, red spider mite. Even more persistent is the root nematode, which can only be seen with a magnifying glass. These can be combatted with systemic insecticides. The true red spider, which is visible to the naked eye, is useful against them, since it eats pests. The presence of 1 to 3 mm long (0.039 to 0.118 inch) woolly plant lice can be detected by the presence of the hairy cocoons in which the young develop. Where these are not numerous, they can be removed with a stream of water or picked off with tweezers, but more heavily infested parts of the plant should be treated immediately with a chemical insecticide. Another pest, the cochineal insect, develops under the protection of a small, round shield, and can be combatted in a manner similar to the woolly plant louse.

## SCIENTIFIC NAMES

Many of the scientific names appearing in this book may strike the uninitiated reader as puzzling—names like *Cylindropuntia subulata* (Mühlf.) Knuth (p. 24). The last two words are examples of notations giving, often abbreviated, the names of the botanists who classified the species or genus, or the authors of standard reference works who use this particular scientific name. It is not necessary for you to know more than the Latin name itself. However, because for many succulent genera, such as *Euphorbia*, *Opuntia*, *Mammillaria*, there is disagreement over names, these additional clues are given for the information of those interested.

At first glance, *Pereskia grandifolia* looks more like a regular plant than a cactus. Only the areoles (cushions in which the spines are based), which are located on the axils of the leaves, indicate that it is a cactus. Pereskias are the most primitively developed cacti. *Pereskia grandifolia,* also known as *Rhodocactus grandifolius* (Haw.) Knuth, is a shrub 1 to 5 metres (3 to 16 feet) high, from Brazil. The leaves, which grow up to 15 cm (6 inches) in length, are cast off in the dry season.

CARE: Since Pereskias are only slightly succulent plants and cannot store up much water, they must be watered regularly. Only large plants bloom. In spite of its beautiful blossoms, *Pereskia grandifolia* is less recommended for the cactus amateur on account of its size and special requirements. Since *Pereskia* thrives in winter, it is popular for use as a grafting stock in the propagation of Zygocactus (see p. 38).

POPULAR NAME: **Rose Cactus**

*Pereskia grandifolia*
Rose Cactus

17

SCIENTIFIC NAME: **Opuntia pycnantha Eng. var. margaritana Coult**

FAMILY: *Cactaceae*

SUBFAMILY: Opuntioideae

Many cacti of the subfamily Opuntioideae have as a primitive characteristic small leaves that have not yet turned into spines and which later fall off. Typical of the Opuntia are glochids—small, barbed bristles which break off easily and are difficult to remove from the skin. The designation fig cactus comes from the fact that the large fruits, also called prickly pears, of many Opuntias are edible. Also, in the Mediterranean region, where *Opuntia ficus-indica* (L) Mill. was introduced, these fruits play an important rôle. The genus *Opuntia* has a great many species. They include large, tree-like species as well as dwarf forms that remain small.

CARE: Most Opuntias bloom well. Since the range of this large genus reaches from Canada to the southern tip of South America, the individual species, although all easy to care for, have different requirements. There are even winter-hardy species which in cool climates, circumstances permitting, can be left in the open to winter over. The branches of the very beautiful *Opuntia pycnantha* grow to 15 cm (6 inches) long. The typical form has yellowish glochids, while the variety *margaritana* has brownish-red ones. The 4 cm ($1\frac{1}{2}$ inch) wide

18

*Opuntia pycnantha* var. *margaritana*
**Prickly Pear**

blossoms of the variety are an intense yellow. Both hail from Lower California in Mexico. *Opuntia pycnantha*, a readily blooming species, needs a lot of light and sunshine. In winter, these plants are best kept not too cool but dry.

POPULAR NAMES: **Prickly Pear, Fig Cactus, Tuna, Cholla**

SCIENTIFIC NAME: *Opuntia microdasys* (Lehm.) Pfeiff. var.
*albispina* Fobe
FAMILY: *Cactaceae*
SUBFAMILY: Opuntioideae

This decorative, spineless *Opuntia* is present in practically every cactus collection. The branches grow to
10 to 15 cm (4 to 6 inches) long. The standard form
has yellow glochids, the variety illustrated has white
ones, and the variety *rufida* K. Sch., reddish-brown
glochids. The variety *albispina* is especially popular,
since its less prickly, especially attractive glochid
clusters contrast with the dark green of the
branches. These remain somewhat smaller than the
main stalk, which grows to 60 cm (24 inches) at the
tallest.
CARE: *Opuntia microdasys*, a warmth-loving plant
from northern Mexico, blooms pale yellow or reddish. Since it is very sensitive to rot, it should be kept
fairly dry at all times. It should winter over cool and
dry.

POPULAR NAME: **Bunny Ears**

*Opuntia microdasys* var. *albispina*
**Bunny Ears**

SCIENTIFIC NAME: **Opuntia bergeriana** Web.
FAMILY: *Cactaceae*
SUBFAMILY: Opuntioideae

The original habitat of *Opuntia begeriana* is unknown. Although it grows wild on the Mediterranean coasts, it was probably brought there from the
Americas by the Spaniards. It grows 3.5 metres ($11\frac{1}{2}$
feet) high; blossoms appear from the time the plant
is a metre (40 inches) high. The single branch grows
to 25 cm (10 inches) long.

CARE: *Opuntia bergeriana* is best kept as a tub plant.
Sufficiently large plants bloom in summer in the
open, with an abundance of blossoms. *Opuntia
bergeriana* must winter over in a frost-free place.

*Opuntia bergeriana*

SCIENTIFIC NAME: *Cylindropuntia subulata* (Mühlf.) Knuth
FAMILY: *Cactaceae*
SUBFAMILY: Opuntioideae (genera *Opuntia* and *Cylindropuntia*)

Although the Cylindropuntias are well differentiated from Opuntias, they are sometimes regarded as a subgenus of *Opuntia*. Backeberg, however, has separated the illustrated species and its relatives from *Cylindropuntia* and has set them up in the new genus *Austrocylindropuntia*. The illustrated species can be recognized by its especially striking leaves, up to 12 cm ($4\frac{3}{4}$ inches) long. In contrast to *Cylindropuntia tunicata* (Lehm.) Knuth, which bristles with spines, it is only weakly protected. *Cylindropuntia subulata*, a shrub growing to a height of 4 metres (13 feet) and having beautiful pinkish-red blossoms, probably originated in northern Argentina and Bolivia, although its original habitat is not known exactly. Blossoms appear only on large plants. Even without them, however, *Cylindropuntia subulata* enriches every cactus collection.

CARE: These plants need nutritious soil and a warm, sunny location. They can also remain in light and warmth in winter, but must be dry.

*Cylindropuntia subulata*

SCIENTIFIC NAME: *Opuntia aciculata* Griff. var. *orbiculata* **Backbg.**
FAMILY: *Cactaceae*
SUBFAMILY: Opuntioideae

Texas is the original home of this *Opuntia*, which is only 1 metre (40 inches) tall and forms a clump up to 3 metres (10 feet) wide. The individual plants in the clump grow from 5 to 12 cm (2 to $4\frac{3}{4}$ inches) long; the orange-brown glochids stay on for several years. The blossoms of the species type are golden yellow and are often green in the middle. The blossoms of the illustrated variety on the contrary identify themselves by their fire-red color. They appear even when the plant is small. The true original habitat of the variety is not known.
CARE: In its cultivation requirements, *Opuntia aciculata* does not differ from other species that are not winter-hardy.

*Opuntia aciculata* var. *orbiculata*

SCIENTIFIC NAME: *Opuntia azurea* Rose
FAMILY: *Cactaceae*
SUBFAMILY: Opuntioideae

This species is considered one of the most beautiful and desirable Opuntias. The round, blue-green-skinned branches reach a diameter of 15 cm (6 inches). The decorative spines, up to 8 cm ($3\frac{1}{8}$ inches) long, develop only on the upper half of the branch. The bicolored blossoms appear readily on young plants, but only on plants with few branches. They are about 6 cm ($2\frac{3}{8}$ inches) across and are often bright red as in the illustrated blossom. The carmine red fruit is edible. *Opuntia azurea* comes from Mexico and the southwestern part of the United States.
CARE: It is cultivated like other non-winter-hardy species.

*Opuntia azurea*

SCIENTIFIC NAME: *Azureocereus hertlingianus* Backbg.
FAMILY: *Cactaceae*
SUBFAMILY: Cactoideae
TRIBE: Browningiae

This column-like cactus from Peru, with its blue or blue-green skin and profuse spines, adds a special touch to the cactus collection. However, we cannot expect blossoms from *Azureocereus hertlingianus* since we can cultivate only young plants in the house. *Azureocereus hertlingianus*, a stalk-building, tree-like cactus, grows to a height of 8 metres (26 feet). The white blossoms, which open only at night, appear only on old plants.

CARE: This cactus requires clay-containing soil (loam) and should be in a warm, sunny location. Only under such conditions will it develop its beautiful, bright-blue color. When wintering over, it needs light and warmth, and must be kept dry.

*Azureocereus hertlingianus*

SCIENTIFIC NAME: *Rhipsalidopsis gaertneri* (Reg.) Lind., **Hybrid**
FAMILY: *Cactaceae*
SUBFAMILY: Cactoideae
TRIBE: Hylocereae

Not all cacti are dwellers in dry, often desert-like regions. Many species have become adapted to the moist living conditions of forests. They live there as do many orchids, Bromelias and ferns, as climbing plants (vines) or as non-parasitic growths on trees (epiphytes). *Rhipsalidopsis gaertneri* is an epiphytic, ramous (many-branched), small bush of the tropical forests of southern Brazil with branches up to 5 cm (2 inches) long, and 2 cm ($\frac{3}{4}$ inch) wide and with blossoms 4 to 5 cm ($1\frac{1}{2}$ to 2 inches) wide. The types found on the market are selected plants as well as cross-breeds with *Rhipsalidopsis rosea* Werderm (Dwarf Easter Cactus).

CARE: They should be kept in conformity with their place of origin—warm, damp (not wet!) and shady and they bloom in March or April in the North Temperate Zone. The best blossom crop is achieved when the plants are kept cool and somewhat drier in the winter.

POPULAR NAME: **Easter Cactus**

*Rhipsalidopsis gaertneri*

**Easter Cactus**

SCIENTIFIC NAME: *Rhipsalis (mesembryanthemoides)*
*mesembrianthoides* **Haw.**
FAMILY: *Cactaceae*
SUBFAMILY: Cactoideae
TRIBE: Hylocereae

The species of the genus *Rhipsalis* live as does
*Rhipsalidopsis*, epiphytically on trees (hence the
popular name Mistletoe Cactus) or on rocks
(lithophytically). It may assume many striking
forms—round, flattened, angular or winged. The
white blossoms are small, but often appear in great
numbers, and the red fruits of several species present
a beautiful sight. These species, such as *Rhipsalis
houlletiana* Lem., really deserve the name of Coral
Cactus. *Rhipsalis* is the only genus of cactus native
to the Old World as well as the New and includes
species from Sri Lanka, Madagascar and Africa.
*Rhipsalis mesembrianthoides*, from Brazil, grows in
a hanging position to a length of 40 cm (16 inches),
and has white fruits.

CARE: The plants should be located in semi-shade
and, like all epiphytes, they are lime-sensitive and
must not dry out. The warmer these plants are kept,
the higher the humidity of the air should be. To get a
better show of blossoms—the blooming period in
the North Temperate Zone begins in Decem-
ber—keep them drier for about 6 to 8 weeks from
the end of September.

POPULAR NAME: **Clumpy Mistletoe Cactus**

*Rhipsalis mesembrianthoides*
**Clumpy Mistletoe Cactus**

SCIENTIFIC NAME: *Epiphyllum x Hybridus, Phyllocactus x Hybridus*
FAMILY: *Cactaceae*
SUBFAMILY: Cactoideae
TRIBE: Hylocereae

In this plant, cactus breeding has achieved its highest point. From plants that were originally difficult to grow and not always disposed to bloom, a diversity of rewarding hybrids has been bred, which bloom splendidly under poor conditions. The modern breeds usually known among us as Phyllo- or Orchid Cactus are derived from the genera *Nopalxochia, Epiphyllum, Heliocereus* and *Selenicereus* and combine the good characteristics of these genera. The illustrated breed belongs to an artificial genus of this kind, and should really be called *x Heliochia*, since the parent plants come from the genera *Heliocereus* and *Nopalxochia*.

CARE: Phyllocacti should not be located in the blazing sun and require lime-free soil rich in nutrients and a relatively large amount of moisture. They winter over best at a temperature of about 10° C. (50° F.) and are kept drier during this time, as well as for a few weeks after blooming stops in midsummer.

POPULAR NAME: **Orchid Cactus**

*Epiphyllum* x *Hybridus*

**Orchid Cactus**

SCIENTIFIC NAME: **Zygocactus truncatus (Haw.) K. Sch., Hybrid**
FAMILY: *Cactaceae*
SUBFAMILY: Cactoideae
TRIBE: Hylocereae

Two wild species are the parent plants of the Christmas cacti, *Zygocactus truncatus* with asymmetric blossoms and *Schlumbergera bridgesii* (Lem.) Lofgr. with uniformly shaped blossoms, which come in many shades of color. Both are epiphytes from the tropical forest of eastern Brazil.
CARE: They have the same cultivation requirements as the other epiphytic cacti. In the Northern Temperate Zone after the beginning of August, keep Christmas cacti cooler and drier so that they can be more profusely watered again in September. By doing this, the plants can be counted on to bloom seasonally at Christmas time.

POPULAR NAMES: **Crab Cactus, Claw Cactus, Christmas Cactus**

*Zygocactus truncatus*
Crab Cactus

SCIENTIFIC NAME: ***Aporocactus flagelliformis*** **(L.) Lem.**
FAMILY: *Cactaceae*
SUBFAMILY: Cactoideae
TRIBE: Hylocereae

The Rat-tail Cactus, a luxuriously blooming cactus, has wide distribution as a hanging plant, especially in rural districts. The asymmetrically formed blossoms, which are strongly reminiscent of *Zygocactus*, appear seasonally in the spring and are 7 to 9 cm ($2\frac{3}{4}$ to $3\frac{1}{2}$ inches) long and last for 3 or 4 days. The snake-like shoots, 1 to 2 cm ($\frac{1}{2}$ to $\frac{3}{4}$ inch) thick grow 100 to 150 cm (40 to 60 inches) long. *Aporocactus flagelliformis* comes from the Mexican mountain country.

CARE: This cactus grows best in loose, humus-rich soil and likes the open sunlight. In its blooming and growth periods, it needs a lot of water and heightened humidity. In winter, it should be kept in a cool, bright place and not completely dry. It is outstandingly suitable for the beginner.

POPULAR NAME: **Rat-tail Cactus**

*Aporocactus flagelliformis*

**Rat-tail Cactus**

SCIENTIFIC NAME: *Hylocereus undatus* (Haw.) Br. & R.
FAMILY: *Cactaceae*
SUBFAMILY: Cactoideae
TRIBE: Hylocereae

Several large-flowered, exclusively night-blooming cacti are called Queen of the Night or Princess of the Night or similar names. In Europe, these are species of the genus *Selenicereus* and regionally also *Echinopsis*, and in the United States the genus *Hylocereus* is so called. The blossoms of *Selenicereus* and *Hylocereus* possess a great deal of similarity. Both genera consist of climbing plants which live epiphytically on trees. The shoots or branches of *Selenicereus* are round, while those of *Hylocereus* are angular. The species illustrated probably comes from Haiti. Its true place of origin is hard to determine, since it has been planted in many tropical countries as splendidly blooming hedges, and in many other places it grows wild. The blossoms are up to 3 metres (10 feet) long, with a diameter of 30 cm (1 foot) and are admired for their size and beauty.

CARE: *Hylocereus undatus*, like *Selenicereus grandiflorus* (L.) Br. & R. requires a lot of nourishment and warmth. Both will also bloom in a somewhat shaded window. *Hylocereus undatus* re-

*Hylocereus undatus*
Honolulu Queen

quires somewhat higher humidity and should winter
over dry and cool (10° C. or more) (50° F.).

POPULAR NAMES: **Honolulu Queen, Night-blooming Cereus**

SCIENTIFIC NAME: *Cereus peruvianus* (L.) Mill. f.
*monstrosus* DC.
FAMILY: *Cactaceae*
SUBFAMILY: Cactoideae
TRIBE: Cereae

The big, tree-like, branched column cactus of the genus *Cereus* in its homeland is often a familiar feature of the landscape. The most stately species reach a height of 15 metres (49 feet). *Cereus peruvianus* grows to only 3 metres (10 feet) in height and, its widespread branches attain a breadth of up to 5 metres (16 feet). It does not come from Peru, as the scientific name might have one think, but from southeastern South America. *Cereus peruvianus* is a species that has many forms. Those known by the name of Curiosity Plants belong to the variety *monstrosus* and are esteemed because of their bizarre appearance. The white blossoms are 10 to 15 cm (4 to 6 inches) long and appear only on old plants. They open only at night.
CARE: *Cereus peruvianus*, a rewarding cactus, should be kept in a place that is warm, bright and airy in the summer and cool in winter. Its slow growth is an advantage for most cactus hobbyists.

POPULAR NAME: **Curiosity Plant**

*Cereus peruvianus*
Curiosity Plant

SCIENTIFIC NAME: *Cephalocereus senilis* (Haw.) Pfeiff
FAMILY: *Cactaceae*
SUBFAMILY: Cactoideae
TRIBE: Pachycereae

The Old Man Cactus as a rule grows without branching. In Mexico plants are found up to 15 metres (49 feet) high and 30 cm (12 inches) in diameter. The yellowish-white, night-opening blossoms do not appear on the plant until it is about 6 metres (over 19 feet) high. Small plants suitable for the hobby grower are recognizable by their thick, white covering of hair.

CARE: Hairy cacti need an occasional light feeding of lime. During the growing season, the Old Man Cactus needs a lot of light, moist heat and close air. It is also sensitive to wetness at this time. The winter temperatures should range around 15° C. (59° F.).

POPULAR NAME: **Old Man Cactus**

*Cephalocereus senilis*

**Old Man Cactus**

SCIENTIFIC NAME: *Acanthocalycium peitscherianum*
**Backbg.**
FAMILY: *Cactaceae*
SUBFAMILY: Cactoideae
TRIBE: Trichocereae

Several species of the genus *Acanthocalycium*,
Argentine cacti that grow in a globular shape, are
characterized by striking pink to lilac-colored
blossoms. In addition to the species illustrated,
*Acanthocalycium violaceum* (Werd.) Backbg. and
*Acanthocalycium spiniflorum* (K. Sch.) Backbg.
should be mentioned here. *Acanthocalycium
peitscherianum* is substantially smaller than the
other two species named. It grows to a breadth of
about 10 cm (4 inches), a height of 8 cm ($3\frac{1}{8}$ inches)
and its blossoms are 6 cm ($2\frac{1}{2}$ inches) long.
CARE: Like its relatives, it is accustomed to extreme
climatic conditions, is undemanding and is a richly
blooming plant. *Acanthocalycium peitscherianum* is
wintered over cool and dry.

*Acanthocalycium peitscherianum*

SCIENTIFIC NAME: *Trichocereus grandiflorus* (Br. & R.) **Backbg.**
FAMILY: *Cactaceae*
SUBFAMILY: Cactoideae
TRIBE: Trichocereae

The Trichocereae of the South American Andes include small species admirably suited to our purposes growing near tree-like plants many metres tall. Most Trichocereae are night bloomers. For day-blooming species, among them *Trichocereus grandiflorus*, Backeberg has proposed the genus name *Heliantho-cereus*, which is not recognized by other authorities. Trichocereae grow well and are popular for use as a grafting stock for difficult cacti. *Trichocereus grandiflorus* grows in small groups. The single columns are at the most 35 cm (14 inches) high and are 6 cm ($2\frac{1}{2}$ inches) through. The blossoms 8 to 10 cm (3 to 4 inches), appear when the plant is only 10 cm (4 inches) tall.
CARE: All Trichocereae are easily satisfied cacti if they are planted in soil rich in nutrients. In summer, they should be kept constantly moist but not wet, in winter cool and dry.

*Trichocereus grandiflorus*

SCIENTIFIC NAME: *Pseudolobivia kermesina* Krainz
*Echinopsis kermesina*
FAMILY: *Cactaceae*
SUBFAMILY: Cactoideae
TRIBE: Trichocereae

The day-blooming species *Pseudolobivia kermesina* is often regarded as a sub-genus of the night-blooming genus *Echinopsis*. For this reason, the species illustrated is also known as *Echinopsis kermesina*. It is a globose cactus seldom more than 15 cm (6 inches) in diameter. The blossoms up to 9 cm ($3\frac{1}{2}$ inches) broad grow to 18 cm (7 inches) long, of which 12 cm (5 inches) consist of a narrow tube. They stay open for three days. The exact origin of *Pseudolobivia kermesina* is unknown, but it probably originated in Argentina.

CARE: *Pseudolobivia kermesina* is a rewarding, free-blooming and easily grown hobbyists' plant. It should be placed in soil containing humus and during its growing period should be kept continually damp—not wet. During winter, it should be kept cool—that is to say, between 5° and 12° C. (41° and 54° F.).

*Pseudolobivia kermesina*

SCIENTIFIC NAME: ***Pseudolobivia aurea* (Br. & R.) Backbg.**
FAMILY: *Cactaceae*
SUBFAMILY: Cactoideae
TRIBE: Trichocereae

Argentina is the original home of this yellow-blooming Pseudolobivia. It grows to a height of 10 cm (4 inches) and develops into either a globular shape or a short cylinder. The size of the blossoms and the width of the petals varies in the different varieties, as well as the length of the spines. The illustrated variety *grandiflora* Backbg. is characterized by its especially wide inner petals and its wheel-like flower-edge.

CARE: The cultivation of *Pseudolobivia aurea* is as free of problems as that of *Pseudolobivia kermesina*. In addition to the wild species, there is a series of easily grown cultivated forms of *Pseudolobivia* and *Echinopsis*.

*Pseudolobivia aurea*

SCIENTIFIC NAME: *Cleistocactus smaragdiflorus* (Web.) Br. & R.

FAMILY: *Cactaceae*

SUBFAMILY: Cactoideae

TRIBE: Trichocereae

Cleistocacti, basically slender, branching, column cacti, have proved to be easy-growing hobbyists' plants. Typical are the long, only partially open, asymmetric blossoms. While the large species are kept on account of their beautiful form and show spines, the small species, one of which is pictured on the opposite page, also please us with their rich show of blossoms. *Cleistocactus smaragdiflorus* from Paraguay and northern Argentina grows partly erect and partly creeping. It grows as long as 100 cm (39 inches) but no thicker than 3 cm (a bit over an inch). It is capable of blooming when it reaches a length of 25 cm (10 inches). It blooms less profusely than many other species of the genus, but the blooming season extends throughout the summer.

CARE: *Cleistocactus smaragdiflorus* requires nutritious soil which should never be allowed to dry out completely during the winter. In its original habitat, it often grows on rocks. *Cleistocactus smaragdiflorus* is especially fond of higher humidity (mist!), especially in the spring and autumn.

POPULAR NAMES: **Firecracker Cactus, Emerald-tipped Cleisto**

*Cleistocactus smaragdiflorus*
**Firecracker Cactus**

SCIENTIFIC NAME: *Borzicactus samaipatanus* (Card.) Kimnach
FAMILY: *Cactaceae*
SUBFAMILY: Cactoideae
TRIBE: Trichocereae

This cactus, known also as *Bolivicereus samaipatanus*, can rightfully claim to be one of the most rewarding and freely blooming column cacti. The column-like stalk only 3.5 to 4 cm (around $1\frac{1}{2}$ inches) wide and, according to the variety, 70 to 150 cm (28 to 59 inches) long, branches at the ground, so that small clusters result. The asymmetric blossoms, 3.5 cm ($1\frac{1}{2}$ inches) long, appear in large number several times during the year. The plants are able to produce blossoms even when quite young. In its Bolivian habitat, *Borzicactus samaipatanus* grows at an altitude of nearly 2,000 metres (6,561 feet). The variety *multiflora* (Card.) Krainz grows only to 50 to 70 cm (19 to 28 inches) long.
CARE: *Borzicactus samaipatanus* prefers a sunny location and must not be kept too cold in winter.

*Borzicactus samaipatanus*

SCIENTIFIC NAME: *Hildewintera aureispina* Ritt. *Winteria aureispina, Winterocereus aureispina*
FAMILY: *Cactaceae*
SUBFAMILY: Cactoideae
TRIBE: Trichocereae

The genus *Hildewintera*, also listed as *Winteria* and *Winterocereus*, is a monotype, which is to say it consists of only one species. *Hildewintera aureispina* grows in branched form on rocks, with the shoots hanging downward. The shoots, up to 150 cm (60 inches) long and 2.5 cm (1 inch) thick, are especially beautiful with their golden-yellow spines. The beautiful blossoms 5 cm (2 inches) across last for several days. They appear several times during the year in large number, even on relatively small specimens, if these are kept warm enough and in bright light. The blossoms of *Hildewintera aureispina* possess a double corolla, the only instance of this in the cactus family.

*Hildewintera aureispina*

SCIENTIFIC NAME: ***Chamaecereus silvestrii*** **(Speg.) Br. & R.**
**Hybrid**
FAMILY: *Cactaceae*
SUBFAMILY: Cactoideae
TRIBE: Trichocereae

Also monotypical is the genus *Chamaecereus*.
*Chamaecereus silvestrii* is one of the best-liked and
most rewarding columnar-growing cacti. The
branches, which are 6 cm ($2\frac{1}{2}$ inches) long at the
most and up to 1.5 cm ($\frac{1}{2}$ inch) thick, build small
clusters by means of basal sprouting. They are richly
adorned by large red blossoms, 5 cm (2 inches) long.
This popular plant from the Argentine highlands is
represented by many cultivated forms. By crossing
with Lobivia, especially *Lobivia famatimensis*, the
range of color of the blossoms is broadened—along
with all shades of red, there are also yellow forms.
CARE: *Chamaecereus silvestrii* is a hardy cactus, but
still is susceptible to red spider, which causes the
stems to become discolored. This cactus requires
nutritious, humus-rich soil and is easily propagated
by means of cuttings. In summer, *Chamaecereus
silvestrii* should be where it is bright and airy—not
windy! In the sun, the branches turn a violet-brown.
In winter, stop watering entirely. A cold, bright and
dry location guarantees a good show of blossoms.
Night temperatures may drop below 0° C. (32° F.).
Provided it is kept completely dry, *Chamaecereus*

62

*Chamaecereus silvestrii*

**Peanut Cactus**

*silvestrii* can withstand temperatures down to −20°
C. (−4° F.).

POPULAR NAME: **Peanut Cactus**

SCIENTIFIC NAME: *Lobivia rebutioides* Backbg.
FAMILY: *Cactaceae*
SUBFAMILY: Cactoideae
TRIBE: Trichocereae

The large South American genus *Lobivia* includes an abundance of beautiful hobbyists' cacti which are distinguished by being easy to grow, free-blooming, small in size and by having beautifully colored blossoms. This cactus is also recommended for the beginner and its popularity is shown by the fact that new species and varieties are constantly being discovered and described. The home of the genus *Lobivia* is in the Andes of Bolivia and northern Argentina. Many species build up small cushions by means of budding. *Lobivia rebutioides* builds up cushions which consist of clusters of only 2 cm ($\frac{3}{4}$ inch) diameter. Its blossoms are double that in length and width. Grafted specimens, of course, are substantially larger. *Lobivia rebutioides* hails from northern Argentina. The species type possesses fire-red blossoms; three of the four varieties have yellow blooms.

CARE: Lobivias need loose, humus-containing soil. In summer, they should be kept in a warm, sunny place but not too dry; in winter, in a cool dry and bright place. Wait until spring to begin watering. Unfortunately, there are a number of unintentional cross-

***Lobivia rebutioides***
**Cob Cactus**

breeds, and it is therefore difficult to obtain pure species.

POPULAR NAME: **Cob Cactus**

SCIENTIFIC NAME: *Lobivia arachnacantha* Buin. & Ritt.
FAMILY: *Cactaceae*
SUBFAMILY: Cactoideae
TRIBE: Trichocereae

This Lobivia also grows by budding. The individual bodies of the plant grow to 4 cm ($\frac{1}{2}$ inch) high and 2 cm ($\frac{3}{4}$ inch) wide. *Lobivia arachnacantha* hails from Bolivia, where it occurs at altitudes of 2,000 metres (6,560 feet). The long blossom tube is an attractive feature of this plant. The variety *torrecillasensis* Hort. europ. differs from the others only by the carmine tinted blossoms of the species.

*Lobivia arachnacantha*

SCIENTIFIC NAME: *Espostoa lanata* (HBK.) Br. & R.
FAMILY: *Cactaceae*
SUBFAMILY: Cactoideae
TRIBE: Trichocereae

This columnar cactus from Peru grows in tree- or candelabrum-form to a height of 4 metres (13 feet). The pale-pink, funnel-shaped blossoms are 6 cm (over 2 inches) long, open at night and grow out laterally from a thick cephalium or woolly cap at the apex. The flowers appear only on plants which are too big for our purposes. In spite of this, *Espostoa lanata* is still quite popular on account of its beautiful covering of hair, which clothes even the seedlings. The different varieties of *Espostoa lanata* differ from each other in the length and the coloration of their spines.

CARE: *Espostoa lanata* should be planted in soil rich in nutrients. During the growing season, it should be placed in a warm, sunny spot and kept slightly but constantly damp—it prefers spraying in the evening. Keep cool and dry in the winter.

POPULAR NAME: **Peruvian Old Man**

*Espostoa lanata*
Peruvian Old Man

SCIENTIFIC NAME: *Sulcorebutia steinbachii* (Werd.) Backbg.
**f. *cristata***
FAMILY: *Cactaceae*
SUBFAMILY: Cactoideae
TRIBE: Trichocereeae

*Sulcorebutia*, a genus closely related to *Rebutia*, consists of only a few species, all of which are natives of the Bolivian Andes. They are small, globular cacti which grow and bloom as easily as do *Lobivia* and *Rebutia*, although their blossoms open later in the year.

*Sulcorebutia steinbachii* inhabits altitudes from 2,500 to 3,000 metres (8,200 to 9,840 feet). It builds up small cushions, the individual bodies being 6 cm (over 2 inches) high at the most and 4 cm (1½ inches) wide. If kept in a sunny place, they will develop within their peripheral spines, blue-black, central spines up to 2.5 cm (1 inch) long. The plant in the illustration does not have these central spines. It is a Cristata or pectinate form (shaped like a rooster's comb), as is often found among cacti. Such plants, instead of growing straight to the tip broaden out to form a crest or comb. Cristata forms happen in nature just as they do in cultivation.

CARE: These cacti need a lot of light. In winter, they should be kept dry and cool but not as cold as *Rebutia*.

**70**

*Sulcorebutia steinbachii*

SCIENTIFIC NAME: ***Rebutia krainziana* Kesselr.**
FAMILY: *Cactaceae*
SUBFAMILY: Cactoideae
TRIBE: Trichocereae

Rebutias rival Lobivias in beauty and ease of cultivation. The same goes for the closely related genera *Aylostera* and *Mediolobivia*, which Buxbaum, as opposed to Backeberg, regards as only a subgenus of, or a synonym for, *Rebutia*. For the cactus hobbyist, in any event, the division into several genera is more convenient. Rebutias inhabit high altitudes of the Andes of Bolivia and northern Argentina, where strong temperature differences between day and night are the rule. For this reason, they are especially hardy plants. Under non-optimal conditions in spring, and many times in the autumn as well, they will surprise their owners with many beautifully colored blossoms. *Rebutia krainziana*, a Bolivian species 5 cm (2 inches) tall at the most and 4 cm ($1\frac{1}{2}$ inches) broad, grows by budding. The blossoms 3 cm (1 inch) long and 4 cm wide, open in the North Temperate Zone in May.

CARE: They can spend the summer in temperate climates in a warm, sunny location, with a higher humidity than normal. In winter, Rebutias are best kept dry, cool and in a bright place. Seedlings only a year old will bloom.

POPULAR NAMES: **Crown Cactus, Pygmy Cactus**

*Rebutia krainziana*
Crown Cactus

73

SCIENTIFIC NAME: *Rebutia xanthocarpa* Backbg. var. *luteirosea* Backbg.
FAMILY: *Cactaceae*
SUBFAMILY: Cactoideae
TRIBE: Trichocereae

This Rebutia from northern Argentina reaches a height of 3 to 4.5 cm (1 to 2 inches)—only in exceptional cases 5 cm (2 inches)—and is a true dwarf cactus. The blossoms 2 cm ($\frac{3}{4}$ inch) long, are indeed noticeably smaller than those of the preceding species, but they appear in large numbers. Stemming from *Rebutia xanthocarpa* are varieties with carmine red, mauve pink, salmon pink and bright reddish purple blossoms.

*Rebutia xanthocarpa* var. *luteirosea*

SCIENTIFIC NAME: ***Rebutia senilis*** **Backbg. var. *kesselringiana* Bewg.**
FAMILY: *Cactaceae*
SUBFAMILY: Cactoideae
TRIBE: Trichocereae

*Rebutia senilis*, 8 cm ($3\frac{1}{8}$ inches) long and 7 cm ($2\frac{3}{4}$ inches) wide, is as numerous in forms as *Rebutia xanthocarpa*. The blossoms of its varieties range from carmine red and orange red through yellow-red to lilac-red and yellow. The variety illustrated is one of the two yellow forms. Also, the spining pattern is changeable. All originated in northern Argentina. The blossoms of the variety *kesselringiana* are, with their diameter of 4.5 cm (2 inches), about 1 cm ($\frac{1}{2}$ inch), wider than those of the carmine red blooming species type. The body of the variety *kesselringiana* is less thickly shrouded in white spines.

*Rebutia senilis* var. *kesselringiana*

SCIENTIFIC NAME: *Rebutia violaciflora* **Backbg.**
FAMILY: *Cactaceae*
SUBFAMILY: Cactoideae
TRIBE: Trichocereae

These dwarfish Rebutias, with a 2-cm ($\frac{3}{4}$-inch) diameter, 5 cm (2 inches) at the most, must not be confused with the similarly blooming variety *violaciflora* of *Rebutia xanthocarpa*. *Rebutia xanthocarpa* has white spines, while *Rebutia violaciflora* has brown spines. The blossoms of *Rebutia violaciflora* grow to 4.5 cm ($1\frac{3}{4}$ inches) long and 4 cm ($1\frac{1}{2}$ inches) wide. As with all Rebutias, they are not located on the crown but much farther down on the side of the plant. The species illustrated hails from northern Argentina. From the same region comes *Rebutia violaciflora* var. *knuthiana* (Backbg.) Don. It blooms carmine red and not bright violet as does the species type.

*Rebutia violaciflora*

SCIENTIFIC NAME: *Aylostera fiebrigii* (Gürke) Backbg.
FAMILY: *Cactaceae*
SUBFAMILY: Cactoideae
TRIBE: Trichocereae

It is difficult to imagine more rewarding or more beautiful cacti than the small, globose *Aylostera* species. They are quite close to *Rebutia* and possess the same merits. The genus *Aylostera* is at home in the high Andes of northern Argentina and southeast Bolivia.

With about 10 species, *Aylostera* is a small genus but a rewarding one to collect, though available in only a few places. Thanks to the small size of the plants, many of them can be cultivated in a restricted space. Characteristic of *Aylostera* is the soft, golden lustre of the red or orange petals. *Aylostera fiebrigii* grows singly or by budding and at the most to 6 cm (2½ inches) tall. The long-tubed blossoms measuring 3.5 cm (1½ inches) appear in great number. *Aylostera fiebrigii* was found in its Bolivian habitat at an altitude of 3,600 metres (11,800 feet).

CARE: The *Aylostera* species are springtime bloomers which also get along well in cool climates out in the open during the warm season. They respond well to higher humidity. They often bloom again in late summer. They should be kept cool in a bright place in winter.

*Aylostera fiebrigii*

SCIENTIFIC NAME: *Aylostera fiebrigii* (Gürke) Backbg. var. *densiseta* Culim.
FAMILY: *Cactaceae*
SUBFAMILY: Cactoideae
TRIBE: Trichocereae

Many cacti characterized as varieties can hardly be differentiated from the original species. Many times, their naming comes more or less from a desire to be able to offer something new. It is different, though, with the variety illustrated. It differs clearly from the species type by its covering of thick white spines. When the plant is in fine condition, the blooms are more orange and less red than shown in the illustration, where the blossoms have just opened. The especially fine, white spines of the illustrated form of the variety *densiseta* is also marketed as *Aylostera muscula*.

*Aylostera fiebrigii* var. *densiseta*

SCIENTIFIC NAME: *Aylostera pulvinosa* (Ritt. & Buin.) **Backbg.**
FAMILY: *Cactaceae*
SUBFAMILY: Cactoideae
TRIBE: Trichocereae

This species, unknown until about 1961, can be counted by the cactus hobbyist as being among the most strikingly beautiful of the new plants. Andean dwarf cacti are often found in limited areas separated by mountain peaks from similar biotopes (environments) and are often hard to find when not in blossom. The isolated areas favor the development of new forms, varieties and species. *Aylostera pulvinosa* builds thick cushions. The individual bodies are 3 cm (over 1 inch) tall, the orange blossoms are 1.8 cm ($\frac{3}{4}$ inch) long and 1.5 cm ($\frac{1}{2}$ inch) wide. The native habitat of this cactus is Bolivia.

POPULAR NAME: **Andean Dwarf Cactus**

*Aylostera pulvinosa*
**Andean Dwarf Cactus**

SCIENTIFIC NAME: ***Aylostera deminuta* (Web.) Backbg. var. *pseudominuscula* (Speg.) Donald**

FAMILY: *Cactaceae*

SUBFAMILY: Cactoideae

TRIBE: Trichocereae

Northern Argentina is the original habitat of this rare, budding *Aylostera*. It grows there at an altitude of 3,500 metres (11,500 feet). The single bodies grow to 5 cm (2 inches) tall and 3.5 cm (1½ inches) wide. The intensely colored blossoms are about 3 cm (1¼ inch) long and wide. As in the other species, they appear low down on the body of the plant.

*Aylostera deminuta* var. *pseudominuscula*

SCIENTIFIC NAME: *Mediolobivia brachyantha* (Wessn.) **Krainz**
FAMILY: *Cactaceae*
SUBFAMILY: Cactoideae
TRIBE: Trichocereae

The Mediolobivias, another genus related to the Rebutias, are also extremely easy plants to grow. The question as to whether or not the genus *Mediolobivia* is justified will not be discussed here. All the species of this genus are easily cared for by the hobbyist—they grow easily and bloom richly. Many of these small, globose or cylindrical cacti build cushions.

*Mediolobivia brachyantha* growing in the shape of a short cylinder reaches a diameter of only 2 cm ($\frac{3}{4}$ inch). Grafted plants, especially, build clumps by budding. The blossoms are up to 2 cm (1 inch) long, in proportion to the size of the body. From the similar *Mediolobivia auranitida* (Wessn.) Krainz, the species illustrated and others differ by their brownish-red, not blackish-green, sprouts. The original habitat of *Mediolobivia brachyantha* is unknown, but is probably Bolivia.

CARE: From summer until the beginning of autumn, Mediolobivias thrive best in a sunny, continually damp location in the open. In winter, they should be kept cool and dry in a bright place.

*Mediolobivia brachyantha*

SCIENTIFIC NAME: ***Mediolobivia aureiflora* Backbg.**
FAMILY: *Cactaceae*
SUBFAMILY: Cactoideae
TRIBE: Trichocereae

From northern Argentina comes *Mediolobivia aureiflora*, a clump-building, very variable species. Backeberg describes seven varieties, three of which possess red blossoms, the remainder yellow. A few varieties, and this goes especially for older plants, are attractive by reason of long, upthrust, central spines. The individual bodies of *Mediolobivia aureiflora* achieve at the most a diameter of 5 to 6 cm (2 to $2\frac{1}{2}$ inches). The blossoms grow to 4 cm ($1\frac{1}{2}$ inches) across. Very similar is the yellow-blooming *Mediolobivia elegans* Backbg., also from northern Argentina.

*Mediolobivia aureiflora*

SCIENTIFIC NAME: *Mediolobivia pygmaea* (R. E. Fries) **Backbg.**
FAMILY: *Cactaceae*
SUBFAMILY: Cactoideae
TRIBE: Trichocereae

This species, also known as *Mediolobivia haagei* (Fric & Schelle), has bi-colored blossoms which attract our special attention. *Mediolobivia pygmaea* grows singly or by budding and in the wild only 1 to 3 cm ($\frac{1}{2}$ to 1 inch) tall and 1.2 to 2 cm ($\frac{1}{2}$ to $\frac{3}{4}$ inch) across. When grafted, cultivated plants grow larger. *Mediolobivia pygmaea* comes from the Andes of northern Argentina. The variety *flavovirens* Backbg. differs from the species type by a yellow-green body color and brown spines in the crown. *Mediolobivia pectinata* Backbg. var. *neosteinmannii* Backbg. possesses similar, bi-colored blossoms.

*Mediolobivia pygmaea*

SCIENTIFIC NAME: ***Mediolobivia ritteri* (Wessn.) Krainz**
FAMILY: *Cactaceae*
SUBFAMILY: Cactoideae
TRIBE: Trichocereae

*Mediolobivia ritteri*, a budding plant with a diameter of 5 cm (2 inches), has blossoms 4 cm (1½ inches) long and 4.5 cm (2 inches) across. The variety *pilifera* (Fric) Backbg. differs by having brighter, almost white spines. This plant grows in Bolivia at an altitude of 3,400 metres (11,000 feet). The true original habitat of the variety is unknown.
CARE: All Mediolobivias are cultivated in the same way as *Mediolobivia brachyantha*.

*Mediolobivia ritteri*

SCIENTIFIC NAME: *Neochilenia esmeraldana* (Ritt.) Backbg.
FAMILY: *Cactaceae*
SUBFAMILY: Cactoideae
TRIBE: Notocacteae

Chile and Argentina are the habitat of several genera of globose cacti, among which are many easy-to-grow hobbyists' plants. Great differences of opinion exist over the classification of genera and species. Actually, *Neochilenia, Chileorebutia, Horridocactus* and *Pyrrhocactus* are closely related to one another. *Neochilenia esmeraldana* was first classified as *Chileorebutia*. It hails from Chile and achieves a diameter of only 5 to 7 cm (2 to 3 inches).

CARE: The cultivation of *Neochilenia esmeraldana*, like most of its relatives, provides no difficulties. It is a slow-growing cactus which, once it settles down, is distinguished by a rich show of blossoms. The plant needs a great deal of warmth and should not be kept too moist. In winter, keep it in a bright place and relatively warm.

*Neochilenia esmeraldana*

SCIENTIFIC NAME: ***Astrophytum myriostigma* Lem.**
FAMILY: *Cactaceae*
SUBFAMILY: Cactoideae
TRIBE: Notocacteae

This cactus from Mexico is known as Bishop's Cap. The usually five-ribbed, often three- to ten-ribbed, spineless body is thickly encrusted with wool-like flakelets which give the plant its unmistakable appearance. Old plants, only by way of exception, may grow 60 cm (24 inches) tall. A whole series of varieties, among them also some without flakelets, reveal the changeability of this cactus.

CARE: *Astrophytum myriostigma* to thrive well needs soil rich in nourishment and lots of sun, but only a little water. In winter, it should be kept—as well as for a few weeks in midsummer—completely dry. Its main growing season occurs in the autumn. Older plants reward this care with many blossoms. Like other hairy cacti, this plant should be given lime occasionally.

POPULAR NAMES: **Bishop's Cap, Star Cactus**

*Astrophytum myriostigma*
Bishop's Cap

SCIENTIFIC NAME: ***Astrophytum capricorne*** **(Dietr.) Br. & R.**
FAMILY: *Cactaceae*
SUBFAMILY: Cactoideae
TRIBE: Notocacteae

Contrary to the foregoing spineless species, *Astrophytum capricorne* possesses a confusion of long spines. It grows to a height of 25 cm (10 inches) and is distinguished by especially beautiful, large blossoms. *Astrophytum capricorne*, of the several forms described, hails from northern Mexico. On account of its symmetrical form, the spineless *Astrophytum asterias* (Zucc.) Lem., the Sea-Urchin Cactus, is especially popular. It is native to Mexico and Texas and grows to about 10 cm (4 inches) wide and 3 cm (1 inch) tall. Strangely striking is the similarity in habit between the Sea-Urchin Cactus and the South African *Euphorbia obesa*. Like all species of the Astrophytum genus, it bears yellow blossoms.

CARE: It is cultivated like *Astrophytum myriostigma*.

POPULAR NAME: **Goat's Horn**

***Astrophytum capricorne***

**Goat's Horn**

SCIENTIFIC NAME: ***Copiapoa montana* Ritt.**
FAMILY: *Cactaceae*
SUBFAMILY: Cactoideae
TRIBE: Notocacteae

The genus *Copiapoa* inhabits the desert region of northern Chile. Imported mature plants usually do not thrive well in cooler climates. However, plants cultivated from seedlings and grafted plants, circumstances permitting, prove their worth as easy-blooming, easy-to-grow plants—which is also the case with very young plants.

*Copiapoa montana*, a species not long known, grows by budding. The individual shoots grow to a height of 20 cm (8 inches) and their diameter runs to 5 to 10 cm (2 to 4 inches). The fragrant blossom is 4 to 5.5 cm ($1\frac{1}{2}$ to 2 inches) wide and 4 cm ($1\frac{1}{2}$ inches) long.

CARE: The main growing season of *Copiapoa* falls in autumn in the North Temperate Zone, for which reason the plants are kept dry in summer and, it goes without saying, in winter also. In the warm season, protect them against burning by placing them in a half-shaded location.

*Copiapoa montana*

SCIENTIFIC NAME: ***Parodia sanguiniflora* Fric ex Backbg.**
FAMILY: *Cactaceae*
SUBFAMILY: Cactoideae
TRIBE: Notocacteae

Parodias, comparatively small, globose cacti from southern Brazil, Bolivia, Paraguay and northern Argentina, possess all the good features a cactus hobbyist could wish for. They require little room, are distinguished by a wonderfully beautiful, wide variety of spining, and readily bring forth blossoms of gleaming color, which often appear in great number on the crown of the plant and last for several days. To occupy oneself with these beautiful cacti is as rewarding for the beginner as it is for the advanced hobbyist. A collection consisting only of Parodias—there are about 40 species in the genus—offers a sight that is rich in variety. *Parodia sanguiniflora* is outstanding because of its deep, blood-red blossoms which rise up strikingly above the bright spines. However, there are also plants with bright red blossoms. *Parodia sanguiniflora* is from northern Argentina and grows to about 8 cm (3 inches) in height. The blossoms, 3 to 4 cm (1 to $1\frac{1}{2}$ inches) in size, often appear in rich profusion.

CARE: Cultivation of Parodia offers no special difficulties, only growing from seeds is not entirely easy. Parodias thrive well in loam into which some humus has been mixed. In the growing and blooming

*Parodia sanguiniflora*
Crimson Tom's Thumb

seasons, they require lots of sunshine, fresh air, and plentiful water. Under no circumstances, however, will they tolerate puddled water. In winter, keep them cool (5° to 10° C.) (41° to 50° F.) and dry.

POPULAR NAME: **Crimson Tom's Thumb**

SCIENTIFIC NAME: ***Parodia mutabilis*** **Backbg.**
FAMILY: *Cactaceae*
SUBFAMILY: Cactoideae
TRIBE: Notocacteae

Changeable, as its scientific name indicates, this Parodia is counted among the best known and most responsive species of the genus. It is not only attractively spined, but also bears an exceptional abundance of blossoms. The throat of the blossom, which grows up to 4 cm ($1\frac{1}{2}$ inches) in size, is tinted pale pink or whitish. The variously described varieties of *Parodia mutabilis* differ from each other largely in size and the color of the central spines. *Parodia mutabilis* is globose and grows to over 8 cm (over 3 inches) in size. It comes from northern Argentina.

*Parodia mutabilis*

SCIENTIFIC NAME: *Parodia saint-paeana* **Backbg.**
FAMILY: *Cactaceae*
SUBFAMILY: Cactoideae
TRIBE: Notocacteae

With its short spines, this decorative, small
Parodia—only 4 to 5 cm (1½ to 2 inches) in size—
stands in striking contrast to the following species,
which is thickly shrouded in spines, and shows the
variety of this genus. *Parodia saint-paeana*, which
comes from northern Argentina, grows by budding.
Its blossoms are comparatively small.

SCIENTIFIC NAME: *Parodia chrysacanthion* (K. Sch.) **Backbg.**
FAMILY: *Cactaceae*
SUBFAMILY: Cactoideae
TRIBE: Notocacteae

This Parodia from northern Argentina, which grows to 8 cm (3¼ inches) tall, has straight instead of hooked central spines. The ribs are studded with warts. The comparatively small blossoms, only 1 to 2 cm (½ to ¾ inch) long, open half-covered up in the woolly crown. In the pattern of its spines, however, *Parodia chrysacanthion* surpasses in beauty many of its relatives.

**109**

SCIENTIFIC NAME: ***Brasilicactus haselbergii*** (Hge.) Backbg.
FAMILY: *Cactaceae*
SUBFAMILY: Cactoideae
TRIBE: Notocacteae

The original habitat of the Brasilicacti lies in southern Brazil and Uruguay. It is so closely related to *Notocactus* that it can also be regarded as a subgenus of that genus. The illustrated species enjoys great popularity, since this beautifully spined cactus also blooms abundantly and easily in the house. *Brasilicactus haselbergii*, from southern Brazil, grows in the shape of a flattened globe, up to 12 cm (5 inches) in diameter. Disturbances of growth on the sunny side cause the crown to grow slantwise. The blossoms are small with a length of only 1.5 cm ($\frac{1}{2}$ inch), but they appear in large numbers in spring. Their color ranges from orange red to fire red.
CARE: *Brasilicactus haselbergii* should be grown in semi-shade and sprayed regularly during the flowering and growing seasons with soft water. In winter, keep it in a bright place, dry and not too cold.

*Brasilicactus haselbergii*

SCIENTIFIC NAME: **Notocactus ottonis** (Lehm.) Berg.
FAMILY: *Cactaceae*
SUBFAMILY: Cactoideae
TRIBE: Notocacteae

All Notocacti are outstandingly suitable for the beginner. They are beautifully spined, globular cacti which grow well and bloom easily. Notocacti, which range from southern Brazil to northern Argentina, also bloom readily as young plants.

*Notocactus ottonis* is a small species from southern Brazil, Uruguay and northern Argentina that is quite variable—Backeberg names 8 varieties. The bodies grow to 5 to 6 cm (2 to $2\frac{1}{2}$ inches) wide. Larger examples of 7 to 11 cm (3 to $4\frac{1}{2}$ inches) diameter are very rare. The blossoms grow to 6 cm ($2\frac{1}{4}$ inches) long and 4 cm ($1\frac{1}{2}$ inches) across. The blooming season of *Notocactus ottonis* extends over the entire summer.

CARE: They grow best in rich soil containing humus and, during the growing season, are kept slightly but uniformly damp. In winter they should be kept in a bright place, dry and not too cold. Do not let them dry out completely. This wintering over guarantees a good show of blossoms.

POPULAR NAME: **Ball Cactus**

***Notocactus ottonis***
**Ball Cactus**

SCIENTIFIC NAME: *Notocactus scopa* (Spreng.) Berg.
FAMILY: *Cactaceae*
SUBFAMILY: Cactoideae
TRIBE: Notocacteae

In contrast to the preceding species, *Notocactus scopa* is an imposing plant with a maximum height of 25 cm (10 inches) and is 10 cm (4 inches) in diameter. It has especially beautiful spines and also has a great deal of charm even when without blossoms. The broad blossoms, 4 cm ($1\frac{1}{2}$ inches) long appear in great number close to the crown. Even small specimens bloom. The different varieties of *Notocactus scopa* differ from one another principally in the color of their spines. The variety *ruberrima* has white outer spines, which contrast effectively with the red central spines of this variety. The variety *daenikerianus* has yellow outer and central spines; the variety *glauserianus*, on the other hand, has yellow outer and orange or brown central spines. *Notocactus scopa* is a cactus of southern Brazil and Uruguay.

POPULAR NAME: **Silver Ball**

*Notocactus scopa*
Silver Ball

SCIENTIFIC NAME: *Notocactus horstii* Ritt.
FAMILY: *Cactaceae*
SUBFAMILY: Cactoideae
TRIBE: Notocacteae

The color of the blossoms of most Notocacti is yellow, with tones of red occurring less frequently. The more sought-after are red and red-orange blooming species such as *Notocactus horstii*, *Notocactus rutilans* Dän. & Krainz and *Notocactus herteri* Werd. The species illustrated is from Uruguay. The globose-to-cylindrical body grows to a height of at most 15 cm (6 inches). The blossoms reach a size of 4 cm (1½ inches). *Notocactus horstii* and *Notocactus herteri* resemble each other very much. *Notocactus herteri*, however, has coarser spines and purplish-red blossoms. In its cultivation requirements, *Notocactus horstii* does not differ from the other species of the genus.

*Notocactus horstii*

FAMILY: *Cactaceae*
SUBFAMILY: Cactoideae
TRIBE: Notocacteae

Typical for all species of this small genus are the sharp-edged ribs and the very woolly crown. *Malacocarpus* can also be considered as a subgenus of *Notocactus*. It is also known by the generic name of *Wigginsia*. The demarcation of species having an abundance of forms is beset with difficulties. *Malacocarpus sessiliflorus* comes from Uruguay and Argentina. It grows to 30 cm (12 inches) at the tallest and 20 cm (8 inches) broad. It grows and blooms easily, like all the species of this genus known to us.

CARE: It is cultivated the same way as *Notocactus*. In winter, move it to a bright, dry place that is not too cold. Unfortunately, in the course of time, the underpart of the plant turns corky.

*Malacocarpus sessiliflorus*

SCIENTIFIC NAME: *Eriocactus leninghausii*  (Hge. jun.)
**Backbg.**
FAMILY: *Cactaceae*
SUBFAMILY: Cactoideae
TRIBE: Notocacteae

Sought after on account of its attractive spining, this beautiful, clump-building species hails from southern Brazil. It also goes under the name *Notocactus leninghausii*. The column-like growth of the body achieves a diameter of 10 cm (4 inches) and a height of up to 100 cm (40 inches). The silkily gleaming yellow blossoms, 5 cm (2 inches) in size, come forth from the wool felt of the slanting crown. They appear as soon as the plant is about 20 cm (8 inches) tall and continue to be conspicuous for a duration of several days.

CARE: *Eriocactus leninghausii* is cultivated like Notocacti. It desires nutritious, humus soil and does well throughout the summer in half-shade, but likes to be kept in a bright place during the winter.

*Eriocactus leninghausii*

SCIENTIFIC NAME: **Melocactus oaxacensis (Br. & R.)**
**Backbg.**
FAMILY: *Cactaceae*
SUBFAMILY: Cactoideae
TRIBE: Notocacteae

The globose Melocacti are among the monotypic (single-species) cacti. In the crown of plants that are ready to bloom is a thick crest of wool, the cephalium, which, in the case of many species, grows bigger along with its plant. The blossoms of Melocacti are small, not very attractive and mostly buried in the cephalium. However, the rest of the plant is attractive enough. Unfortunately, these desirable plants are tricky to grow and not recommended for the beginner.

CARE: They desire a bright, warm place with a higher humidity and for this reason are best kept in summer under glass. In winter, they should be kept in a bright, cool place. They must not be allowed to dry out completely. *Melocactus oaxacensis* from Mexico, with a diameter of 12 to 15 cm (5 to 6 inches), belong to the small species of the genus. The cephalium grows only 2 to 3 cm ($\frac{3}{4}$ to 1 inch) high. The color of the blossoms is a dark pink.

*Melocactus oaxacensis*

123

SCIENTIFIC NAME: **Weingartia neocumingii** Backbg.
FAMILY: *Cactaceae*
SUBFAMILY: Cactoideae
TRIBE: Notocacteae

This undemanding, abundantly blooming cactus is favored by beginners as well as experienced cactus hobbyists. The plant grows singly and at first globose, reaching a breadth of 10 cm (4 inches) and a height of 20 cm (8 inches); the blossoms grow to a length of 2.5 cm (1 inch). The genus *Weingartia* is classified by some authors as a subgenus of *Gymnocalycium*. Its original habitat is unknown, but it probably hails from Peru.

CARE: Ungrafted plants thrive best in abundantly nutritious, humus soil. In winter, *Weingartia neocumingii* should be kept in a bright place at not too low a temperature and completely dry.

*Weingartia neocumingii*

SCIENTIFIC NAME: *Gymnocalycium baldianum* **Speg.**
FAMILY: *Cactaceae*
SUBFAMILY: Cactoideae
TRIBE: Notocacteae

South American genus *Gymnocalycium* contains a large number of extremely rewarding and popular species. They are for the most part globose cacti that remain small, and readily produce large, often pleasingly colored blossoms. They grow quickly and present no particular difficulties in cultivation. With the wild forms are associated a large number of cross-breeds and involuntary hybridizations. *Gymnocalycium baldianum* is attractive by reason of the intense red of its blossoms. Ungrafted, it achieves a diameter of 7 cm ($2\frac{3}{4}$ inches) and a height of 8 cm ($3\frac{1}{8}$ inches). Its habitat is Argentina. The blossoms grow to 4.5 cm (2 inches) in size and appear even on young plants.

CARE: *Gymnocalycium baldianum*, like all the species of the genus, belongs in nutritious soil that is rich in humus. It thrives as well in semi-shade as in the sun. Low winter temperatures make no difference to it.

POPULAR NAME: *Gymnocalycium* species are called **Chin Cacti.**

**126**

*Gymnocalycium baldianum*
Chin Cacti

127

SCIENTIFIC NAME: ***Gymnocalycium artigas* Hert.**
FAMILY: *Cactaceae*
SUBFAMILY: Cactoideae
TRIBE: Notocacteae

Yellow blossoms are found in the genus *Gymnocalycium* much more frequently than red. The blossoms of *Gymnocalycium artigas*, 3 cm (1 inch) long, a small, globose cactus from Uruguay, measuring only 8 cm ($3\frac{1}{8}$ inches), are a more intense yellow than those of many related species. They are monosexual, a rare occurrence among cacti. That is, the stigma in the male blossom and the anther in the female are rudimentary. The white wool of the areoles of these beautifully spined plants contrasts effectively with the dark green of the plant body. *Gymnocalycium artigas* for this reason also looks attractive when it is not bearing blossoms.

*Gymnocalycium artigas*

SCIENTIFIC NAME: *Gymnocalycium calochlorum* (Böd.) Y. Ito
FAMILY: *Cactaceae*
SUBFAMILY: Cactoideae
TRIBE: Notocacteae

This cushion-building *Gymnocalycium* is a species that is quite variable in the color of its blossoms. This is especially true of the illustrated variety *proliferum* (Backbg.) Backbg. n. comb. The inner petals of the blossoms can be brownish-white to pink or pure white; the throat may or may not have a beautiful pinkish glimmer. The blossoms of *Gymnocalycium calochlorum* are 5 to 6 cm (2 to $2\frac{1}{2}$ inches) long, those of the variety *proliferum* being still longer. The individual body achieves a diameter of 5 cm (2 inches) at the most. Argentina is the habitat of the original form as well as of the variety illustrated.

*Gymnocalycium calochlorum*

SCIENTIFIC NAME: *Gymnocalycium mihanovichii* (Fric et Gürke) Br. & R. var. *friedrichii* Werd. forma *rubra*
FAMILY: *Cactaceae*
SUBFAMILY: Cactoideae
TRIBE: Notocacteae

The red mutation of this variety of *Gymnocalycium mihanovichii* was discovered among many seedlings in 1941 and propagated by a Japanese cactus breeder. Since it possesses no chlorophyll, it cannot manufacture its own food. For this reason, it thrives only when grafted. Associated with the red mutation have also been brown and yellow forms, cacti which awaken the interest of every flower lover. On a good stock, these even develop large, pinkish blossoms 6 cm (2½ inches) in length and 4.5 cm (2 inches) across. They widely surpass in beauty the whitish-green blossoms of the original cactus species. *Gymnocalycium mihanovichii*, alone of the four varieties described here, hails from Paraguay. With a diameter of at most 6 cm (2½ inches), it grows only slightly taller than 3 cm (1 inch).
CARE: The illustrated red form of the variety *friedrichii* keeps its beautiful color best in a bright location.

POPULAR NAME: **Rose-plaid Cactus**

*Gymnocalycium mihanovichii* var. *friedrichii*
**Rose-plaid Cactus**

SCIENTIFIC NAME: *Echinocereus subinermis* SD
FAMILY: *Cactaceae*
SUBFAMILY: Cactoideae
TRIBE: Echinocereae

The genus *Echinocereus*, from the southwestern United States and Mexico, contains an abundance of rewarding hobbyists' plants. They are low, often creeping, cacti with soft-fleshed columns which often build large clumps through budding. The showy blossoms are in marked distinction to those of many other cacti by the longer time they last on the plant. The typical green pistil shows up in attractive contrast to the colorful flower petals.

*Echinocereus subinermis* is a very weak or generally spineless species from Mexico which grows globose at first, later, however, columnar and is little inclined to bud. It grows to 10 to 15 cm (4 to 6 inches) high and 7 to 9 cm (3 to $3\frac{1}{2}$ inches) wide. Unfortunately, it blooms less readily than other species.

CARE: In their growing season, Echinocereus needs lots of light and warmth as well as a comparative abundance of water. This applies in special measure to the weakly spined species and therefore also to *Echinocereus subinermis*. The more thickly spined or haired Echinocereus are more sensitive to

**134**

*Echinocereus subinermis*

**Hedgehog Cactus**

moisture and must be watered with care. In winter, keep all cool, dry and in a bright place. In summer, they thrive well in the open.

POPULAR NAME: **Hedgehog Cactus**

SCIENTIFIC NAME: ***Echinocereus fitchii*** **Br. & R.**
FAMILY: *Cactaceae*
SUBFAMILY: Cactoideae
TRIBE: Echinocereae

This highly popular species of the genus *Echinocereus* comes from Texas. It is a prettily blooming cactus in the shape of a short cylinder which grows to 8 to 10 cm (3 to 4 inches) tall and 4 to 5 cm ($1\frac{1}{2}$ to 2 inches) wide. In contrast to the preceding species, the ribs are thickly spined. The dark throat lends a special touch to the blossom, which may grow to a breadth of 9 cm ($3\frac{1}{2}$ inches).
CARE: It should be watered with care. That is, avoid getting water on the spines.

*Echinocereus fitchii*

SCIENTIFIC NAME: *Echinocereus websterianus* G. Lindsay
FAMILY: *Cactaceae*
SUBFAMILY: Cactoideae
TRIBE: Echinocereae

With its column 60 cm (24 inches) tall and 8 cm ($3\frac{1}{8}$ inches) wide, this wide-ranging, clump-building, Mexican *Echinocereus* belongs among the most splendid representatives of the genus, which includes about 70 species. The ribs, totalling 12 to 18, are thickly spined. The blossoms, which appear even on relatively small plants, are about 6 cm ($2\frac{1}{2}$ inches) long.

*Echinocereus websterianus*

SCIENTIFIC NAME: *Roseocactus kotschoubeyanus* (Lem.)
Berg. *Ariocarpus kotschoubeyanus* (Lem.) Berg.
FAMILY: *Cactaceae*
SUBFAMILY: Cactoideae
TRIBE: Cacteae

This plant bears witness once again to the many
shapes existing among cacti. The spineless warts
arranged in rosettes are more remindful of the succulent leaves of an aloe than of a cactus. In blossom-
less condition, the defenceless plant hardly rises
above its stony surroundings. A tender wool felt
lines the furrows between the warts. Being but 4 to 5
cm ($1\frac{1}{2}$ to 2 inches) in height, it belongs among the
dwarf cacti. The blossoms, nevertheless, are 3 cm
(more than 1 inch) long, which is relatively very
large. *Roseocactus kotschoubeyanus* has a long,
turnip-like root and is usually grafted. It comes from
central Mexico.
CARE: It likes sun and in winter should be kept cool
and completely dry.

*Roseocactus kotschoubeyanus*

SCIENTIFIC NAME: **Echinocactus grusonii** Hildm.
FAMILY: *Cactaceae*
SUBFAMILY: Cactoideae
TRIBE: Cacteae

This plant, native to central Mexico, is attractive by reason of its beautiful spining and symmetrical growth. The relatively small, yellow blossoms appear in the woolly crown of older plants which, as a rule, are already too large for a home collection. *Echinocactus grusonii* first grows in the shape of a flattened globe, then later into a short cylinder. It develops up to 80 cm (over 30 inches) wide at the most and 130 cm (over 50 inches) high. Since, like all the species of the genus *Echinocactus*, it grows rather slowly, it can be recommended for a collection in a cramped space.

CARE: It requires a lot of warmth, is very sensitive to standing wetness and should be protected against sunburn. Winter temperatures must not drop below 10° C. (50° F.). During this time, watering should not be altogether discontinued.

POPULAR NAMES: **Golden Barrel Cactus, Bisnaga, Bisnagita**

*Echinocactus grusonii*
Golden Barrel Cactus

SCIENTIFIC NAME: *Hamatocactus setispinus* (Eng.) Br. & R.
FAMILY: *Cactaceae*
SUBFAMILY: Cactoideae
TRIBE: Cacteae

*Hamatocactus setispinus* is one of the most rewarding of cacti. It thrives in a window location and blooms while still a young plant. The blossoms open one after the other during the time from May to November in North Temperate climate. Even without blossoms, *Hamatocactus setispinus* still has a very decorative appearance. Its range of distribution reaches from northern Mexico to southern Texas. Another similarly rewarding specimen is *Hamatocactus hamatocanthus* (Mühlpf.) Knuth., which is native to approximately the same region. It is conspicuous by reason of its longer spines and also has yellow blossoms. *Hamatocactus setispinus* grows to 15 cm (6 inches) tall, *Hamatocactus hamatocanthus* to 60 cm (24 inches).

CARE: *Hamatocactus setispinus* should be planted in rich soil. It thrives in full sunlight and should not be watered too abundantly. In winter, keep it dry but not too cool.

POPULAR NAME: **Strawberry Cactus**

*Hamatocactus setispinus*
**Strawberry Cactus**

145

SCIENTIFIC NAME: *Echinofossulocactus xiphacanthus* Miqu.
FAMILY: *Cactaceae*
SUBFAMILY: Cactoideae
TRIBE: Cacteae

Typical of the Mexican globular cacti of the genus *Echinofossulocactus* is the large number—often 30 to 60—of narrow, wavy ribs. The central spine of many species is broadened out like a leaf. Equally striking is the bi-colored blossom, seldom found among cacti. Unfortunately, classification of the very changeable species is fraught with difficulties. *Echinofossulocactus xiphacanthus* is also considered a form of *Echinofossulocactus arrigens* (LK.) Br. & R. It grows to about 12 to 13 cm (5 inches) high and possesses many narrow central spines, like many of its relatives. All are rewarding, easy-blooming species for the beginner, the blossoms of which open seasonally in the spring.

CARE: *Echinofossulocactus* species like a bright, semi-shaded location. In summer, their water requirement is rather large. In winter, keep them not entirely dry and not too cool.

*Echinofossulocactus xiphacanthus*

SCIENTIFIC NAME: *Ferocactus latispinus* (Haw.) Br. & R.
FAMILY: *Cactaceae*
SUBFAMILY: Cactoideae
TRIBE: Cacteae

Ferocacti are kept principally for their handsome spines. Although many species grow 3 metres (10 feet) tall in their native land, there is no reason not to keep Ferocacti, since these plants grow very slowly. Some Ferocacti, such as *Ferocactus acanthodes* (Lem.) Br. & R., which grows to 3 metres (10 feet) tall, are clad in a gleaming dress of red spines. The species illustrated is distinguished by central spines strongly widened out to resemble leaves. It grows only to 40 cm (16 inches) high and comes from Mexico. Color and breadth of the spines are very changeable within the species. The variety *flavispinus*, for example, has yellow instead of reddish-brown spines. The pretty pink to purplish blossoms appear only on old specimens.

CARE: Ferocacti are not particularly sensitive, but like to be kept in a warm, sunny place. In winter, keep them dry and relatively warm (around 15° C. or 59° F.).

POPULAR NAME: Fish-hook Barrel Cactus

*Ferocactus latispinus*
Fish-hook Barrel Cactus

SCIENTIFIC NAME: *Mammillaria hahniana* **Werd.**
FAMILY: *Cactaceae*
SUBFAMILY: Cactoideae
TRIBE: Cacteae

The genus *Mammillaria* includes about 300 species and therefore is the largest cactus genus. In spite of many common characteristics, its species are so rich in variations that it is worthwhile to collect them systematically. In addition to the blooming season, we can also enjoy the abundant spining of this hardy plant. Most Mammillarias bloom readily in spring and summer. Since, however, there are also winter bloomers among them, a skilfully put together collection can produce a show of blossoms over a long period of time. The red fruits decorate many species for a long time after that. An important advantage of Mammillarias is their small size, so that even a large collection requires only a small space. It is no wonder, then, that Mammillarias are among the most popular and widespread cacti, even among non-specialized hobbyists.

*Mammillaria hahniana* attracts attention to itself by reason of its long, white hair. It stands in effective contrast to the red blossoms arranged in a wreath around the crown, which, as is the case with all Mammillaria, grow out of the axils and not out of the areoles. It grows by budding or sprouting and builds small groups. The globose at first, then cylin-

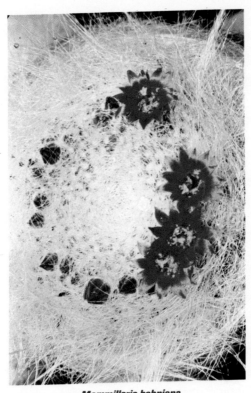

*Mammillaria hahniana*
Old Lady Cactus

drical, plants grow to about 10 cm (4 inches) tall. *Mammillaria hahniana* is a mountain plant from Mexico and is not suitable for the beginner.

CARE: The cultivation of most species calls for no special difficulties. In winter, they are usually kept dry. *Mammillaria hahniana* should not winter over in a place that is too cool. A rest period of several weeks in summer, during which time it is barely watered, is especially good for it.

POPULAR NAME: **Old Lady Cactus**

SCIENTIFIC NAME: ***Mammillaria swinglei*** **(Br. & R.) Böd.**
FAMILY: *Cactaceae*
SUBFAMILY: Cactoideae
TRIBE: Cacteae

This Mammillaria has a height of 10 to 20 cm (4 to 8 inches) and is beautifully furnished with big, campanulate (bell-shaped) blossoms. It grows singly or by budding and differs from *Mammillaria sheldonii* (Br. & R.) Böd. only by the presence of axillary bristles. Both come from Mexico and are perhaps only different forms of the same species. *Mammillaria swinglei* also develops forms which are less thickly haired than the illustrated example. In any case, both *Mammillaria swinglei* and *Mammillaria*

*Mammillaria swinglei*

*sheldonii* with their bi-colored blossoms provide a charming accent in every Mammillaria collection.

SCIENTIFIC NAME: *Mammillaria hidalgensis* J. A. Purp.
FAMILY: *Cactaceae*
SUBFAMILY: Cactoideae
TRIBE: Cacteae

This wart cactus from the Mexican state of Hidalgo is attractive because of the dark green body, which is first round, and later club-shaped. It is among the most popular species and it has a special value for the hobbyist, since it does not bloom in the spring like most Mammillarias, but in late summer.

CARE: *Mammillaria hidalgensis* grows well and blooms readily but should be located where it is protected from the full glare of the sun. The plant grows to 10 cm (4 inches) high and 6 to 8 cm ($2\frac{1}{2}$ to 3 inches) wide.

POPULAR NAME: **Wart Cactus**

*Mammillaria hidalgensis*
**Wart Cactus**

SCIENTIFIC NAME: **Mammillaria prolifera (Mill.) Haw.**
FAMILY: *Cactaceae*
SUBFAMILY: Cactoideae
TRIBE: Cacteae

*Mammillaria prolifera*—illustrated is the variety *texana* (Engelmann) Krainz. comb. nov.—is still more popular and less demanding than the preceding species. It is esteemed for the beautiful red fruits which decorate the plant over a long period of time. *Mammillaria prolifera* is a thickly budding, cushion-building cactus with separate heads 4 to 6 cm ($1\frac{1}{2}$ to $2\frac{1}{2}$ inches) long. There are varieties with white, yellow and brown spining. This species is abundant in forms and hails from Mexico, Texas, Cuba and Haiti.

*Mammillaria prolifera*

SCIENTIFIC NAME: **Mammillaria bocasana** Pos.
FAMILY: *Cactaceae*
SUBFAMILY: Cactoideae
TRIBE: Cacteae

This is another undemanding Mammillaria which can be recommended to every beginner, a cactus whose beautiful covering of spines affords a charming sight. The hook-shaped, usually brown, central spines offer a wonderfully beautiful contrast with the fine, white bristle-spines which thickly shroud the body. *Mammillaria bocasana* grows without difficulties and blooms readily. It is a plant which is rather variable in its spining. There is also a form with yellow instead of brown central spines. It grows singly or by budding (sprouting) and can form thick cushions. The length of the individual body achieves 4 to 5 cm ($1\frac{1}{2}$ to 2 inches). The red, gleaming fruits up to 4 cm ($1\frac{1}{2}$ inch) long decorate the plant for months at a time. *Mammillaria bocasana* comes from Mexico.

POPULAR NAME: **Powder Puff Cactus**

*Mammillaria bocasana*
Powder Puff Cactus

SCIENTIFIC NAME: *Mammillaria zeilmanniana* **Böd.**
FAMILY: *Cactaceae*
SUBFAMILY: Cactoideae
TRIBE: Cacteae

*Mammillaria zeilmanniana* from Mexico is just as undemanding and ready-blooming as *Mammillaria bocasana*. It grows singly, occasionally budding, and attains a diameter of 5 to 6 cm (2 to $2\frac{1}{2}$ inches). The rest period takes place at the same time as most of the rest of them, but not all species of the genus *Mammillaria* rest in winter. Recently, a white-blooming form of *Mammillaria zeilmanniana* has been offered.

*Mammillaria zeilmanniana*

SCIENTIFIC NAME: ***Mammillaria centricirrha* Lem.**
FAMILY: *Cactaceae*
SUBFAMILY: Cactoideae
TRIBE: Cacteae

Characteristic of *Mammillaria centricirrha* and a series of similar species from Mexico are the big, angular warts and the woolly axils. With a height of 12 to a maximum of 20 cm (5 to 8 inches), this Mammillaria that sprouts from beneath belongs among the larger species of the genus. It therefore requires somewhat more room than the two species described just previously. The differentiation of the species and subspecies of Mammillaria provides great difficulties and many species and subspecies have more than one widely accepted name. The different subspecies of *Mammillaria centricirrha* demonstrate the variability of this species. The rather similar *Mammillaria magnimamma* Haw. possesses, in contrast to the species illustrated, yellowish blossoms with weak red stripes in the middle.

CARE: *Mammillaria centricirrha* can winter over somewhat cooler than the previously described species.

*Mammillaria centricirrha*

SCIENTIFIC NAME: *Leptocladodia elongata* DC. *Mammillaria elongata*
FAMILY: *Cactaceae*
SUBFAMILY: Cactoideae
TRIBE: Cacteae

This abundantly sprouting, clump-building cactus is also known as *Mammillaria elongata*. A group of several members of this beautifully spined plant makes a fine ornament even without blossoms, and it has a place among the most popular cacti for beginners. The diameter of the columnar heads of *Leptocladodia elongata*, which grows up to 20 cm (8 inches) long, may reach to 3.5 cm ($1\frac{1}{2}$ inches). Its blossoms are bright yellow. It comes from Mexico and is a variable species, of which many differently spined varieties have been described.

CARE: *Leptocladodia elongata* thrives best in soil rich in nourishment. Water carefully in summer and in winter keep in a cool place and do not water at all.

POPULAR NAME: **Golden Stars**

*Leptocladodia elongata*
Golden Stars

SCIENTIFIC NAME: *Lophophora williamsii* (Le. ex SD.) Coult
FAMILY: *Cactaceae*
SUBFAMILY: Cactoideae
TRIBE: Cacteae

The region of distribution of this spineless cactus reaches from central Mexico to southern Texas. It grows 5 to 8 cm (2 to $3\frac{1}{8}$ inches) wide and has a long, vigorous, turnip-like root. *Lophophora williamsii* is a quite variable species. As a rule, the blossoms are pink and less often white as in the illustrated plant. The defenceless, fleshy body of this cactus contains, as a protection against being eaten by animals, various alkaloids, of which mescaline, a strong narcotic, is the most important. It causes hallucinations similar to LSD, but also causes nausea and vomiting. In ancient Mexico, the plant (called peyote) played an important rôle in cult festivals and even today the Indians use mescaline, which is also contained in other species of the genus, as a narcotic.

CARE: It should be planted in soil rich in nutrients and minerals; in summer, water it moderately and in winter, keep it dry. Given the right care, it blooms readily.


POPULAR NAME: **Peyote**

*Lophophora williamsii*
Peyote

SCIENTIFIC NAME: *Dolichothele longimamma* (DC.) Br. & R.
FAMILY: *Cactaceae*
SUBFAMILY: Cactoideae
TRIBE: Cacteae

The genus *Dolichothele* is closely related to *Mammillaria*. All the species dealt with here are just as rewarding hobby plants as the one under discussion. The especially attractive species illustrated possesses strikingly long warts and is distinguished by blossoms 5 to 7 cm (2 to 3 inches) long. The *Dolichothele longimamma* 8 to 15 cm (3 to 6 inches) in size, hails from Mexico. It grows singly or builds groups by budding and has a large, turnip-like root.

CARE: *Dolichothele longimamma*, like all the species of the genus, should be kept in semi-shade in summer and not too dry. It is, however, very sensitive to wetness. In winter, keep it dry and not too cool. During its rest season, the soft-fleshed body shrivels up.

POPULAR NAME: **Finger-mound Cactus**

***Dolichothele longimamma***
**Finger–mound Cactus**

SCIENTIFIC NAME: *Coryphantha clavata* **(Scheidw.) Backbg.**
FAMILY: *Cactaceae*
SUBFAMILY: Cactoideae
TRIBE: Cacteae

This species also dealt with under the name of *Coryphantha raphidacantha*, is not identical with *Coryphantha clava* (Pfeiff.) Lem. *Coryphantha clavata* hails from Mexico, where it grows in the shape of a club to cylindrical and achieves a diameter of 4 to 7 cm ($1\frac{1}{2}$ to 3 inches). All *Coryphantha* species desire a very sunny location. *Coryphantha clavata* grows well and blooms quite readily when it is old enough. In the axils can be discovered red nectar glands, which are sought after by ants. These glands are missing on some species of the genus.

CARE: The columnar Coryphantha, to which the illustrated species belongs, must be kept not too dry during its growing season. In winter, however, it is not to be watered at all. It can then withstand very low temperatures.

POPULAR NAME: **Pincushions**

*Coryphantha clavata*
**Pincushions**

SCIENTIFIC NAME: **Turbinicarpus lophophoroides** (Werd.) **Buxb. & Backbg.**

FAMILY: *Cactaceae*

SUBFAMILY: Cactoideae

TRIBE: Cacteae

As its scientific name indicates, this Mexican globose cactus is similar in habit to *Lophophora*, but is spined. There are various opinions as to which genus the illustrated species belongs to, whether to *Turbinicarpus, Toumeya* or *Strombocactus*, respectively, and whether *Turbinicarpus* is only a subgenus of *Toumeya. Turbinicarpus lophophoroides* grows only 3.5 cm ($1\frac{1}{2}$ inches) high and 4.5 cm (2 inches) wide. It has large, turnip-like roots. Since, like its relatives, it grows slowly, it is preferably grafted.

CARE: It is more difficult to cultivate than most Mammillarias, to which it is closely related. In any case, it belongs in a warm, sunny location. During the growing season, it should be kept quite moist; in winter, cool and dry.

172

*Turbinicarpus lophophoroides*

SCIENTIFIC NAME: *Euphorbia milii* **Des Moulin var. splendens** (Boj. ex Hook.) Ursch et Lean.

FAMILY: *Euphorbiaceae*, Spurge Family

The Spurge Family contains a great number of stemmed succulents. Many are similar in habit to cacti, to which, however, they bear no close relationship. This is revealed by the completely different kind of blossom, whose splendor cannot be equalled by cactus blooms. The bizarre forms of Euphorbia, however, are no less impressive than the cacti. Of the 2,000 species of the genus *Euphorbia*, several hundred are succulents. In the Old World, they inhabit terrain similar to the terrain where cacti thrive in America.

*Euphorbia milii* var. *splendens*, the Crown of Thorns, hails from Madagascar. It blooms untiringly and its gleaming red bracteoles, 1 cm ($\frac{1}{2}$ inch) in size, which surround the unimpressive inflorescence (blossom cluster), can be enjoyed practically throughout the entire year on a window sill. There are also varieties of *Euphorbia milii*, a species very rich in forms, with yellow and white cyathophylla. The variety illustrated grows to 2 metres ($6\frac{1}{2}$ feet) high.

CARE: The Crown of Thorns likes a bright, sunny place in summer. During its winter rest period, it is best kept quite dry in a bright, not too cool location.

POPULAR NAME: **Crown of Thorns**

*Euphorbia milii* var. *splendens*
Crown of Thorns

SCIENTIFIC NAME: **_Euphorbia obesa_ Hook.**
FAMILY: _Euphorbiaceae_

The convergence of many cacti and Euphorbias, the development of similar life forms and adaptation to similar living conditions, is astounding. The cactus _Astrophytum asterias_ so closely resembles _Euphorbia obesa_ that the one may be mistaken for the other. _Euphorbia obesa_, a highly succulent South African species from the Cape Province, is dioecious (having male and female flowers on separate plants). It grows 8 to 12 cm (3 to 5 inches) across; its blossoms are unimpressive. Unfortunately, it is scarce.

CARE: It should be kept in a warm, bright place in summer. In winter, it should be kept cool and dry.

POPULAR NAMES: **Turkish Temple, Baseball Plant**

*Euphorbia obesa*
Turkish Temple

SCIENTIFIC NAME: *Euphorbia horrida* Boiss.
FAMILY: *Euphorbiaceae*

This heavily spined spurge of the Cape Province very closely resembles a cactus. The thorns are woody, and grow on the not fully developed stems of the inflorescences. *Euphorbia horrida* first grows globose, then later, at a thickness of 20 cm (8 inches), it increases its height to about 1 to 1.5 metres (3 to 5 feet) tall. Small groups are built up by means of budding. As with all species of the genus, the inflorescences of united blossoms called *cyathi* are very unprepossessing. They have green nectar glands.

CARE: *Euphorbia horrida*, a warmth-loving plant, should be kept in a bright, warm place in summer. In winter, it is best kept dry and cool.

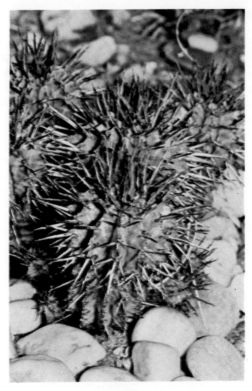

*Euphorbia horrida*

SCIENTIFIC NAME: *Euphorbia aphylla* Brouss.
FAMILY: *Euphorbiaceae*

The Canary Islands are the homeland of this low, thickly branched bush, up to 50 cm (19 inches) high, which builds up large stands of growth in a few places near the coast. *Euphorbia aphylla* possesses no conspicuous cyathophyllae (bracteoles). The visitor to the Islands, however, is far more attracted to the magnificent, 2-metre ($6\frac{1}{2}$-feet) tall thickets of *Euphorbia canariensis* L. Both species can easily be cultivated in the home, since they grow very slowly. *Euphorbia aphylla* is well suited for house-plant culture and can be easily brought up from seed.

CARE: If these plants are to winter over in a cool place, they must be kept dry.

*Euphorbia aphylla*

SCIENTIFIC NAME: ***Euphorbia grandicornis*** Goebel
FAMILY: *Euphorbiaceae*

The forests of the east African coast from Kenya to
Natal are the habitat of these bizarre Euphorbias.
Three triangular branches sprout from a low stalk,
and are set with thorns 3 to 5 cm (1 to 2 inches)
long. *Euphorbia grandicornis* grows to a height of 1
to 2 metres (3 to 6 feet). It possesses large, green
cyathi and dark red fruits which almost completely
cover the upper part of the branches. On account of
its characteristic form, *Euphorbia grandicornis*,
even without blossoms or fruit, forms a high point in
every collection of succulents. Propagation by
cuttings is the best way to success.

CARE: *Euphorbia grandicornis* can be kept warm the
year round, but in summer, its natural rest period,
water it less. On the other hand, it can also winter
over in a cool place.

POPULAR NAME: **Cow-horn Euphorbia**

*Euphorbia grandicornis*
Cow-horn Euphorbia

SCIENTIFIC NAME: *Euphorbia lactea* Haw.
FAMILY: *Euphorbiaceae*

Most succulent species of the genus *Euphorbia* come
from Africa. The range of these succulents, however,
is much larger, extending from Madagascar to India
and even in South America there are a few succulent
Euphorbias. *Euphorbia lactea*, one of the best
known Indian species, is nowadays planted in many
tropical and subtropical countries as a decorative
shrub, and grows wild on the Caribbean islands and
in Florida. Thanks to its beautiful, milk-white mark-
ings, it is a valuable enrichment for a collection of
succulents. *Euphorbia lactea* grows to a height of 3
metres (10 feet), but it grows slowly, so that it can be
enjoyed for a long time. Its milky sap is poisonous.
CARE: Keep *Euphorbia lactea* like the preceding
species, from tepid to warm throughout the year. A
bright location is important in winter.

POPULAR NAMES: **Candelabra Plant, Candelabra Cactus,
Hatrack Cactus, Dragon Bones**

*Euphorbia lactea*
Candelabra Plant

SCIENTIFIC NAME: *Euphorbia pugniformis* **Boiss.** *Euphorbia caput-medusae*
FAMILY: *Euphorbiaceae*

The Euphorbias of the sections *Medusae* and *Pseudomedusae* are attractive because of their curious growth, which has given rise to the Latin name Medusa's-head. From the short, partly buried main stem sprout lateral branches which seem to writhe on the ground like snakes. The lateral branches of the *Pseudomedusae* section, to which the illustrated species belongs, renew themselves after a few years. The lateral branches of *Euphorbia pugniformis*, a plant from the African Cape Province, grow 3 cm (1 inch) long in the wild, but 20 cm (8 inches) long when cultivated. *Euphorbia woodii* N. E. Br. is very similar. The illustrated species is covered with yellowish-green cyathi. The small leaflets can be discerned on the tips of the lateral branches.

CARE: The cultivation of *Euphorbia pugniformis* and its relatives is quite uncomplicated. As a plant native to a coastal region, it should not be kept too dry. It can winter over either warm or cool.

POPULAR NAME: **Medusa's Head**

*Euphorbia pugniformis*
Medusa's Head

SCIENTIFIC NAME: *Jatropha podagrica* **Hook**
FAMILY: *Euphorbiaceae*

In contradistinction to *Euphorbia*, the genus *Jatropha* possesses normally constructed blossoms. In addition to ordinary shrubs and trees, the genus includes a few succulent-stemmed species, among them the illustrated *Jatropha podagrica* from tropical Central America. Seen today in all tropical regions as a garden plant, this popular species possess a bottle-shaped stem, 30 cm (12 inches) tall, that is completely bare during its rest season. The large, 3- to 5-lobed leaves and the inflorescence up to 50 cm (20 inches) high, do not appear until the rainy season. *Jatropha podagrica* belongs in sandy-loam soil.

CARE: It prefers a warm location, but does not withstand the full glare of the sun. In its rest period, after casting its leaves, *Jatropha podagrica* should be kept completely dry.

POPULAR NAME: **Tartogo**

*Jatropha podagrica*
Tartogo

189

SCIENTIFIC NAME: *Kalanchoe pumila* **Bak.**
FAMILY: *Crassulaceae*, Orpine Family

The Orpine family consists principally of leaf-succulents. Stem-succulent species are rare. Many Crassulaceae are rewarding house plants whose characteristic growth and often splendid blossoms have contributed much to their popularity. In addition to the well-known species such as the "Flaming Catkin" *(Kalanchoe blossfeldiana* v. Poelln.) and the "African Monkey-Bread Tree" (*Crassula portulacea* Lam.), there is a large number of lesser known species which exercise a special power of attraction for the collector of succulents. Kalanchoe blooms as a rule in winter; its blooming period is, however, strongly influenced by the shortness of the days. Orpines are easily propagated by means of cuttings or offsets (especially the Kalanchoe). *Kalanchoe pumila* is a dwarf shrub that grows to a height of 10, 20 or at the most 30 cm (4, 8 or at the most 12 inches). It is thickly ramified with attractive, floury-looking leaves and handsome blossoms. It hails from the dry forests of Madagascar.
CARE: While the species with unfrosted leaves can be kept in the open in summer, *Kalanchoe pumila* is better placed under glass. Kalanchoes should be

*Kalanchoe pumila*
Dwarf Purple Kalanchoe

kept cool in winter but not cold. *Kalanchoe pumila* needs soil rich in humus and should be in a bright, airy place. The leaves must not be wetted in watering.

POPULAR NAME: **Dwarf Purple Kalanchoe**

SCIENTIFIC NAME: ***Crassula socialis* Schoenl.**
FAMILY: *Crassulaceae*

The close-pressed, triangular leaves arranged in a rosette lend the sod-building South African *Crassula socialis* an unmistakable appearance. It grows only 6 to 7 cm ($2\frac{1}{2}$ to 3 inches) high. The quite drab, white blossoms appear from February on. *Crassula socialis* remains small, but it grows well and is suitable for a hanging flower pot.

CARE: It needs ground rich in nutrients and, like all succulent species of the genus *Crassula*, it should winter over in a cool, bright place.

*Crassula socialis*

SCIENTIFIC NAME: *Crassula lactea* Sol.
FAMILY: *Crassulaceae*

This 30 to 60 cm (12 to 24 inches) tall, richly bloom-ing subshrub comes from South Africa, the heart of the distribution range of the succulent *Crassula* species.

CARE: In summer, it is best kept in the open; it will then bloom with great abundance in winter.

POPULAR NAME: **Tailor's Patch**

SCIENTIFIC NAME: *Kalanchoe manginii* **Hamet et Perr.**
FAMILY: *Crassulaceae*

Southern Madagascar is the habitat of this pretty Kalanchoe. The woody branches of this leaf-succulent, hanging pot-plant grow 10 to 30 cm (4 to 12 inches) long. The lantern-like blossoms are 2.5 cm (1 inch) long, and appear from January to March.

CARE: *Kalanchoe manginii* is cultivated the same way as *Kalanchoe pumila*. Bright, cool and quite dry wintering over is the best preparation for a good show of blossoms. *Kalanchoe manginii*, can be propagated by offsets as well as by cuttings.

SCIENTIFIC NAME: *Echeveria derenbergii* **J. A. Purp.**
FAMILY: *Crassulaceae*

The habitat of the genus *Echeveria* ranges from Mexico to as far as central Peru. Plants of this genus are leaf-succulents with beautifully colored blossoms. Since, as a rule, they do not grow too large, and are easily cultivated, many of them are rewarding hobby plants. Some species, including the illustrated one, are being cultivated in great quantity, while others that are no less attractive are unjustly less well known. Many cultivated types have been developed from the wild form. *Echeveria derenbergii* is a turf-forming plant from the Mexican mountain country in the state of Oaxaca. It forms small rosettes from 3 to 5 cm (1 to 2 inches) in diameter. The inflorescence, only 8 cm ($3\frac{1}{8}$ inches) high, bears individual blossoms 11 to 15 cm (4 to 6 inches) long. CARE: *Echeveria derenbergii* grows especially well in summer if placed in a sunny spot in the open. In winter, it should be kept in a bright place, cool and quite dry. Water must not be allowed to stand in the middle of the rosette, otherwise, rot sets in all too easily.

POPULAR NAMES: **Painted Lady, Baby Echeveria**

*Echeveria derenbergii*
Painted Lady

SCIENTIFIC NAME: **Sedum morganianum E. Walth.**
FAMILY: *Crassulaceae*

The genus *Sedum*, which is subtropical but also represented in central Europe, consists of about 500 species popularly called stonecrops or live-forevers.

*Sedum morganianum* from Mexico is a thickly-leaved, perennial plant outstandingly suitable for planting in a hanging pot. It grows more than 30 cm (12 inches) long, and the leaves measure about 2 cm ($\frac{3}{4}$ inch). The color of the blossoms ranges from bright pink to dark scarlet-red.

CARE: *Sedum morganianum* is cultivated like *Echeveria derenbergii* with a wintertime, dry rest period. The cast-off leaves are used for propagating. By placing the leaves on wet sand in a propagating frame, or even on ordinary potting soil, tiny plantlets will sprout from the notches in the leaf and take root. When these are large enough, they can be transplanted to pots of their own. Some related genera, such as Kalanchoe, even produce plantlets around the rim of each leaf while the leaf is attached to the plant. These little plants develop roots that hang down into the air! When the plantlets reach a certain size they become detached from the leaf, fall to the ground and take root. Such asexual reproduction is called cloning.

POPULAR NAME: **Burro Tail**

*Sedum morganianum*
Burro Tail

SCIENTIFIC NAME: *Aeonium tabulaeforme* **(Haw.) Webb. et Berth.**

FAMILY: *Crassulaceae*

The flat or almost stemless, plate-like rosettes of *Aeonium tabulaeforme* make this plant, even without blossoms, among the most decorative of succulents. *Aeonium tabulaeforme* hails from Tenerife, in the Canary Islands, where it settles in colonies on steep cliffs. The diameter of the flat rosette can measure up to 50 cm (20 inches). On the 60-cm (24-inch) high abundantly branched inflorescence many small, sulphur-yellow, individual blossoms open. After blossoming, the plant dies; however, it is easily propagated by means of seeds.

CARE: *Aeonium tabulaeforme* is well suited for house-plant culture. It should stand in a bright place, but not in the full glare of the sun. In summer, it thrives best in a suitable place in the open. To winter over keep *Aeonium tabulaeforme* cool (not under 10° C. or 50° F.) and in a bright place. During this time, water quite sparingly.

POPULAR NAME: **Saucer Plant**

***Aeonium tabulaeforme***
**Saucer Plant**

SCIENTIFIC NAME: *Aeonium arboreum* Webb. et Berth. var. *atropurpureum* (Nich.) Brgr.
FAMILY: *Crassulaceae*

In contrast to the preceding species, *Aeonium arboreum* readily withstands full sun. The leaves of the original type are green, those of the illustrated variety show the purplish-red color at its most beautiful, incident to a sunny location. Typical of this species from the Mediterranean region is the stalk that grows to a height of a metre (40 inches) with scarcely any branching. The individual rosettes can reach a diameter of 20 cm (8 inches). On the inflorescence, 20 to 30 cm (8 to 12 inches) tall, develop close-packed clusters of small, yellow, individual blossoms.

CARE: Aside from a location in the open sun, *Aeonium arboreum* is cared for in the same way as *Aeonium tabulaeforme*. The variety or cultivated form *albovariegatum* (West) Boom has whitish-green leaves; the variety *luteovariegatum* (West) Boom has leaves with whitish-yellow stripes.

POPULAR NAME: **Black Tree Aeonium**

*Aeonium arboreum* var. *atropurpureum*
Black Tree Aeonium

SCIENTIFIC NAME: ***Othonna euphorbioides*** **Hutchins**
FAMILY: *Compositae*, Daisy Family

The Composites or Daisy family include succulent species adapted to extremely dry climatic zones. *Othonna euphorbioides*, a heavily armed, stem-succulent, dwarf shrub only 10 to 15 cm (4 to 6 inches) tall, comes from South Africa. The illustrated plant, photographed in summer, has already cast its leaves, since the vegetation period of *Othonna euphorbioides* falls in winter, which is the rainy season in South Africa.

CARE: It must not be watered during its summer rest period.

POPULAR NAME: **Ragwort Vine**

*Othonna euphorbioides*
Ragwort Vine

SCIENTIFIC NAME: *Adenium obesum* (Forsk.) Roem. et Schult.

FAMILY: *Apocynaceae*, Dogbane Family

Among succulents that are still not well known among hobby growers is *Adenium obesum*, an East African stem-succulent, popular today throughout the tropics as an ornamental plant. *Adenium obesum*, grows to a height of 2 to 5 metres ($6\frac{1}{2}$ to 16 feet), while the stem reaches a diameter of almost one metre (40 inches). The milky sap of *Adenium obesum* is very poisonous. Since the plants bloom while still young, they are good as house plants. The seeds, which can be collected, for example, on an East African safari, develop shrubs capable of blooming in three to four years.

CARE: This plant should be kept in a sunny place in summer and abundantly watered. In winter, when the plant has cast off its leaves, keep it quite dry.

POPULAR NAMES: **Impala Lily, Desert Rose**

*Adenium obesum*
Impala Lily

SCIENTIFIC NAME: *Pachypodium lameri* Drake
FAMILY: *Apocynaceae*

Better known than Adenium is another stem-
succulent dogbane, of the thorn-armed genus
*Pachypodium. Pachypodium lameri* grows as a tree
in Madagascar from 1 to 6 metres (3 to 20 feet)
high, with a barrel-shaped trunk 60 cm (24 inches) in
diameter. Young plants are well worth recom-
mending as house plants. Unfortunately, only the
larger specimens bloom, and these are too big for
house plants. Species that remain small, like another
from Madagascar, *Pachypodium rosulatum*,
however, bloom while still in the young stage.
*Pachypodium lameri* has handsome white blossoms
and *Pachypodium rosulatum* beautiful yellow ones.
CARE: Pachypodia thrive excellently in a window.
They easily withstand the dry air of centrally-heated
houses, but like a bright, sunny location. Since they
grow in winter in the North Temperate Zone, they
must be kept drier in summer there.

POPULAR NAMES: **Clubfoot, Madagascar Palm**

*Pachypodium lameri*
Clubfoot

SCIENTIFIC NAME: *Pelargonium tetragonum* L'Her.
FAMILY: *Geraniaceae*, Geranium Family

These close relatives of the well-known *Pelargonium zonale* (L.) Ait., the geranium, have three- to four-edged succulent stems. It grows to 70 cm (28 inches) tall and must be supported in culture, since the stems break off easily. *Pelargonium tetragonum* is from South Africa.

CARE: It should be in a bright, sunny place. Many South African plants rest during the dry summer of their homeland. Like *Pelargonium tetragonum*, they do not adapt themselves to the reversal of seasons in the North Temperate Zone, and they put in their rest period during the summer. During the rest season, water *Pelargonium tetragonum* very little. *Pelargonium tetragonum* can be easily propagated by cuttings.

POPULAR NAMES: **Storksbill, Florists' Geranium**

*Pelargonium tetragonum*
Storksbill

SCIENTIFIC NAME: *Stapelia variegata* L.
FAMILY: *Asclepidaceae*, Milkweed Family

The Milkweed family contains a large number of stem-succulent genera and species, whose beautiful blossoms are not a bit less attractive than those of cacti. The largest blossoms are exhibited by the genus *Stapelia*. The only disadvantage of some Stapelia species is their carrion aroma, which attracts flies and other insects. The little columnar stalk is reminiscent of certain succulent Euphorbias or cacti. On the edges of the leafless stems are so-called teeth. More than 20 varieties of *Stapelia variegata*, a species with an abundance of forms from the Cape Province, have been described, which differ from each other mainly in the shape and color of their blossoms.

The illustrated variety *picta* (J. Donn.) N. E. Br. is a great deal similar to the original form. The little stalk of *Stapelia variegata* grows 5 to 10 cm (2 to 4 inches) high. Having a diameter of 5 to 8 cm (2 to 3 inches), the blossom is relatively small.

CARE: Stapelias root flat, and should be planted in flat dishes and nutritious, loamy soil. The blossoms appear in summer and autumn on the new shoots. In summer, Stapelias require a lot of warmth; in winter they should be kept cool (under 12° C. or 53.6° F.) and given very little water. They are sensitive to

*Stapelia variegata*
Spotted Toad Cactus

strong, direct sunlight. During the growing season, fertilize repeatedly with potash magnesium. Best results in propagation are achieved by severing the shoots (cuttings).

POPULAR NAMES: **Spotted Toad Cactus, Carrion Flower**

SCIENTIFIC NAME: ***Stapelia gigantea*** **N. E. Br.**
FAMILY: *Asclepidaceae*

With a maximum diameter of nearly 40 cm (16 inches), *Stapelia gigantea* possesses the largest of all Stapelia blossoms. The large buds, as with all species of the genus, burst with a clearly heard sound. The little stalks grow to 20 cm (8 inches) high and 3 cm (more than 1 inch) in diameter. The range of this plant, which is also a popular garden plant in Africa, extends from the South African province of Natal to southern Rhodesia.
CARE: *Stapelia gigantea* is cared for in the same way as *Stapelia variegata*.

POPULAR NAMES: **Zulu Giant, Giant Toad Plant**

*Stapelia gigantea*
Zulu Giant

SCIENTIFIC NAME: *Stapelia grandiflora* **Mass.**
FAMILY: *Asclepidaceae*

The eastern part of the Cape Province and the Transvaal in South Africa are the homeland of this abundantly haired species. The shoot, 20 to 30 cm (4 to 12 inches) high, grows 3 to 4 cm (1 to $1\frac{1}{2}$ inches) in diameter. The deeply forked blossoms reach a diameter of 15 to 16 cm (6 to $6\frac{1}{2}$ inches). Its similarity to the somewhat smaller *Stapelia ambigua* Mass. is so great that even the expert has difficulty with the determination. The abundance of forms of many *Stapelia* species makes separating them difficult, and add to this the hybrids which unexpectedly arise in cultivation.

*Stapelia grandiflora*

SCIENTIFIC NAME: *Stapelia longipes* K. Luckh.
FAMILY: *Asclepidaceae*

This ornamental Stapelia comes from southwestern Africa. The sprouts, 5 to 12 cm (2 to 5 inches) tall, form thick clumps up to 40 cm (16 inches) in diameter. The rather small blossoms of 6 cm ($2\frac{1}{2}$ inches) diameter appear on a stem up to 18 cm (7 inches) in length. For this reason, they usually lie upon the ground.

CARE: *Stapelia longipes* is cared for the same as *Stapelia variegata*, yet it does have a greater preference for warmth.

*Stapelia longipes*

SCIENTIFIC NAME: *Huernia pendula* E. A. Bruce
FAMILY: *Asclepidaceae*

The relatives of the Stapelias include many highly interesting, and extensive genera, of which only four can be considered here. Many of the about 50 species of the genus *Huernia* possess just as beautiful, though also smaller, blossoms as Stapelia, to which they are similar in habit. *Huernia pendula* is an exception to the rule on account of its hanging growth. On the irregularly branched shoots 45 to 150 cm (18 to 60 inches) long, are branches 9 cm (3½ inches) long. On a single inflorescence appear from one to four blossoms.

CARE: *Huernia pendula* comes from the Cape Province of South Africa. Like *Stapelia*, it should be kept warm in summer and not too moist; in winter, on the other hand, it should be kept cold and practically dry.

*Huernia pendula*

SCIENTIFIC NAME: *Echidnopsis cereiformis* Hook.
FAMILY: *Asclepidaceae*

*Echidnopsis cereiformis*, native to Ethiopia, Somalia and Southern Arabia, belongs among the best known and most rewarding relatives of *Stapelia*. The plant is 15 to 30 cm (6 to 12 inches) high and 1.5 to 2.5 cm ($\frac{1}{2}$ to 1 inch) thick. From summer to fall, very pretty blossoms appear, only 1 cm ($\frac{1}{2}$ inch) in size, often in great number. The variety *Obscura* Bgr. has brown blossoms and the variety *Brunnea* Bgr. yellowish-brown blossoms.

CARE: *Echidnopsis cereiformis* thrives better than most other succulents of the Milkweed family in a warm, semi-shaded place in an unfinished window. *Echidnopsis cereiformis* should be moderately watered in summer and in winter it is best kept cool and quite dry.

*Echidnopsis cereiformis*

SCIENTIFIC NAME: *Decabelone barklyi* Dyer. *Tavaresia barklyi*

FAMILY: *Asclepidaceae*

The Decabelones of southern and southwestern Africa, also known under the genus name of *Tavaresia*, are very attractive because of their large, funnel-shaped blossoms. Unfortunately, they are suitable only for the experienced cultivator of succulent plants. What is more, they have only recently been grafted on *Ceropegia* stock. *Decabelone barklyi* is native to the Cape Province and southwestern Africa. The stalks grow 7 to 12 cm (3 to 5 inches) tall and over 2 cm ($\frac{3}{4}$ inch) in diameter. The length of the blossom measures 5 to 7 cm (2 to 3 inches). The blossoms of the very similar *Decabelone grandiflora* K. Schum. reach a length of 9 to 14 cm (4 to $5\frac{1}{2}$ inches).

CARE: In summer, they require a great deal of sun, warmth and fresh air, while in winter they should be kept cool and practically dry. Thus, they must be watered very, very little. On account of the short life span of *Decabelone barklyi* and its relatives, they are propagated seasonally by means of seeds.

POPULAR NAME: **Thimble Flower**

*Decabelone barklyi*
**Thimble Flower**

SCIENTIFIC NAME: *Hoodia bainii* Dyer.
FAMILY: *Asclepidaceae*

The cultivation of the highly succulent, South African *Hoodia* species is attended by considerable difficulties similar to those of *Decabelone*. The beautiful, often very large, blossoms are, however, worth the trouble. *Hoodia bainii* is quite similar to *Stapelia* in habit. *Hoodia bainii*, probably the best-known species of the genus, is native to the dry regions of the Cape Province and southwestern Africa. It grows 15 to 40 cm (6 to 16 inches) tall and forms bushy groups. The diameter of the blossom measures 7 cm (3 inches). Other species of the genus grow even larger. *Hoodia gordonii* (Mass.) Sweet. grows to over 1 metre (40 inches) tall. Its blossoms have a diameter of 10 cm (4 inches). Many relatives of Stapelia worthy of being recommended are found in the genera *Caralluma, Duvalia, Trichocaulon* and *Ceropegia*.

CARE: Plants adapted to more extreme dryness require a lot of warmth and sun and must also be very carefully watered in summer. In winter, they are kept completely dry.

*Hoodia bainii*

SCIENTIFIC NAME: **Glottiphyllum depressum** (Haw.) N.E. Br.

FAMILY: *Aizoaceae (Mesembryanthemaceae)*, Carpet-Weed Family

The Carpet-Weed Family offers us an abundance of beautiful and rewarding leaf succulents that are not to be taken in at a glance. Only a few of the most important can be introduced here. The family consists of about 150 genera with over 2,000 species. Almost all are from southern Africa. Many open their blossoms only when the sun stands at its highest. Most highly succulent carpet weeds are small and take up only a little room in their requirements. The easily blooming *Glottiphyllum depressum*, on the other hand, spreads out rapidly and for this reason, in the interest of other plants, it must be tightly reined in. The leaves of *Glottiphyllum depressum* grow 10 cm (4 inches) long and 2 cm ($\frac{3}{4}$ inch) wide. The yellow blossoms reach a diameter of 5.5 cm (more than 2 inches). The plant blooms tirelessly throughout the fall and winter and the individual blossoms are retained for a long time.

CARE: *Glottiphyllum depressum*, a flower of the Cape Province, should be in a sunny place in soil poor in nutritive material and in the growing season should be watered only moderately. In winter, keep it cool and practically dry.

POPULAR NAME: **Tongue Leaf**

*Glottiphyllum depressum*
Tongue Leaf

SCIENTIFIC NAME: *Lithops salicola* L. Bol.
FAMILY: *Aizoaceae*

The species of the genus *Lithops* have completely adapted to life in the desert-like dry regions of South Africa. The highly succulent leaves look like the stones of their surroundings and so protect the plant from being eaten by animals. For this reason, they are also called Living Stones. Evaporation is brought down to a minimum, since the plant is buried in the ground to the upper surface of its leaves. Light should fall upon them only through a window. Since light must pass through the water-storing tissues before it can reach the assimilating tissues on the inner side of the leaves, it arrives there weakened. The individual bodies of *Lithops salicola* grow 2 to 2.5 cm ($\frac{3}{4}$ to 1 inch) high and 1.6 cm ($\frac{1}{2}$ inch) wide, the diameter of the blossoms measures 2.5 cm (1 inch). The plant is native to the Orange Free State.

CARE: In the summertime period of growth, water the warmth-loving *Lithops salicola* carefully. From September on, keep it completely dry. The blossoms appear in the autumn and at the beginning of winter. Wintering over succeeds best in a bright and airy location at about 15° C. (59° F.). *Lithops salicola* can also winter over if kept warm.

POPULAR NAME: **Stoneface**

*Lithops salicola*
Stoneface

SCIENTIFIC NAME: *Pleiospilos nelii* Schwant.
FAMILY: *Aizoaceae*

The comparatively large species of the genus *Pleiospilos* are as completely adapted as *Lithops* to their environment, the dry regions of South Africa. Their leaves are stone-like, hence the name Living Granite. *Pleiospilos nelii* has leaves with a diameter of 7 cm (3 inches). In contradistinction to other species of the genus, the blossoms of *Pleiospilos nelii* often do not appear until spring.

CARE: During its growing season, which falls in the months of May and June in the North Temperate Zone, it should be kept in a warm sunny place and, during this time, should be watered in relative abundance. In its rest season, it is to be kept completely dry. In no case should watering be started up again too soon.

POPULAR NAMES: Cleft Stone, Living Granite

*Pleiospilos nelii*
Cleft Stone

SCIENTIFIC NAME: ***Pleiospilos bolusii*** (Hook. f.) N. E. Br.
FAMILY: *Aizoaceae*

This species, also native to the Cape Province, resembles the preceding one. Its body, 4 to 7 cm (1½ to 3 inches) long, however, does not have the shape of a hemisphere. The golden-yellow blossom reaches the impressive diameter of 6 to 8 cm (2 to 3 inches). It appears in the autumn and lasts for about a week. Though the plant is conspicuous when in flower, it is hard to find in its native land outside the blooming season.

CARE: It is cared for the same as *Pleiospilos nelii* and propagated by seed. Unfortunately, undesirable hybrids or cross-breeds of various species of the genus have appeared again and again in culture.

POPULAR NAME: **Living Rock Cactus**

*Pleiospilos bolusii*
Living Rock Cactus

SCIENTIFIC NAME: *Faucaria felina* (Haw.) Schwant.
FAMILY: *Aizoaceae*

The species *Faucaria* from the Cape Province of South Africa includes about 30 highly succulent carpet-weed plants, the leaf edges of which species are set with teeth, so that they are remindful of the jaw of a beast of prey and hence give the plant its various names of Catjaws, Wolfjaws, and Tigerjaws.

*Faucaria felina* has small, low-stemmed rosettes composed of 2 to 4 pairs of leaves, which later form cushions by branching. The leaves grow 4.5 cm (2 inches) long and 1.5 to 2 cm ($\frac{1}{2}$ to $\frac{3}{4}$ inch) wide. The blossoms appear in the autumn and open in the afternoon. Their diameter measures 5 cm (2 inches).
CARE: Like all species of the genus, *Faucaria felina* should be kept warm in a quite sunny place. In winter, keep it cool and dry. Unfortunately, we often get hold of a hybrid instead of the pure species.

POPULAR NAME: **Catjaws, Wolfjaws, Tigerjaws**

*Faucaria felina*
Catjaws

FAMILY: *Aizoaceae*

Among the 300 species of the genus *Conophytum* are to be found many rewarding leaf-succulents which tempt one as much by the singularity of their bodies as by the beauty of their blossoms. Although for the most part they form small cushions, these dwarf plants require little in the way of extra care. Since Conophytum does not adapt to the rhythm of the seasons in the Northern Hemisphere, its resting season falls in northern summer and its growing period in northern winter. At the beginning of the resting season, the bodies gradually shrivel up, leaving only a paper-like skin. From this husk two new bodies develop during the vegetation period, i.e. in autumn or winter, which, in many species such as *Conophytum wettsteinii* from the Cape Province of South Africa, grow together, closing the small fissure separating them.

The turf-building (ground-cover forming) *Conophytum wettsteinii* bodies grow 1.5 cm ($\frac{1}{2}$ inch) high and 2.2 to 3 cm ($\frac{3}{4}$ to 1 inch) wide. The diameter of the blossoms measures 2 cm ($\frac{3}{4}$ inch). Unfortunately, *Conophytum wettsteinii* is rare.

CARE: Conophytes need a lot of light and warmth but should not be set out in the full glare of the sun. They should also be very carefully watered during

*Conophytum wettsteinii*
**Cone Plants**

the growing season, generally not watered at all during the rest season. They can be cultivated well in a bright place in a window.

POPULAR NAME: Conophytum species are called **Cone Plants**

SCIENTIFIC NAME: ***Conophytum elishae*** **(N. E. Br.) N. E. Br.**
FAMILY: *Aizoaceae*

This Conophytum, also a turf-builder, comes from the Cape Province of South Africa, like the preceding specimen. It grows 2.5 cm (1 inch) high, 1.4 cm ($\frac{1}{2}$ inch) wide and 1 to 1.2 cm (about $\frac{1}{2}$ inch) thick. The diameter of the blossoms measures 2 cm ($\frac{3}{4}$ inch). A deep cleft in the body divides the plant into two lobes.

CARE: *Conophytum elishae* is cultivated in the same way as *Conophytum wettsteinii*. Very similar is *Conophytum meyerae* Schwant.

*Conophytum elishae*

SCIENTIFIC NAME: *Fenestraria rhopalophylla* **(Schltr. et Diels) N. E. Br.**
FAMILY: *Aizoaceae*

The genus *Fenestraria*, native to the Cape Province, consists of only two species, which possess a transparent window similar to *Lithops*. Like many *Lithops* species, *Fenestraria* also grows so deep in sandy soil that only the leaf surface provided with the window is to be seen. In spite of this, to avoid damage from rot, it should not be planted deep in the substratum. Since *Fenestraria*, in contrast to *Conophytum*, does adapt itself to the rhythm of seasons in the Northern Hemisphere, its growing season falls in northern summer. *Fenestraria rhopalophylla* forms a cushion of about 10 cm (4 inches) diameter. The succulent leaves grow to about 2 cm ($\frac{3}{4}$ inch) long, the blossoms 1.8 to 3 cm ($\frac{3}{4}$ to 1 inch) across. The somewhat larger, golden-yellow-flowered *Fenestraria aurantiaca* N. E. Br. provides blossoms from 3 to 7 cm (1 to 3 inches) across.

CARE: Both species should be in a bright place. Also, water very carefully in the growing season. In winter, they should be kept cool (around 12° C. or 53.6° F.) and completely dry.

POPULAR NAME: **Baby Toes**

*Fenestraria rhopalophylla*

**Baby Toes**

SCIENTIFIC NAME: **Haworthia greenii Bak.**
FAMILY: *Liliaceae*, Lily Family

The Haworthia leaf succulents of southern Africa are attractive because of their beautiful habit, or mode of growth. This lily relative, which usually remains small, forms thickly leaved rosettes. The clump-forming *Haworthia greenii* hails from the Cape Province. It grows 15 to 20 cm (6 to 8 inches) high; its leaves grow 3 to 4 cm (1 to $1\frac{1}{2}$ inches) long. The unimpressive white blossoms appear in a loose cluster. *Haworthia greenii* grows first erect but later lies on the ground. The similar *Haworthia reinwardtii* S. D. Haw., a species with an abundance of forms, is often cultivated under the name of *Haworthia greenii*.

CARE: Care of Haworthia offers no special difficulties. In spring and summer, it should be in a semi-shaded location. Strong action of the sun causes a change of color in the leaves, to a reddish hue. In summer, their actual rest period, they are kept quite dry. In autumn and winter, mostly from September to November in the North Temperate Zone, they require more moisture. During this time, they should be kept in a bright place that is not too warm. As with cactus, however, they can be allowed to sprout in summer and to winter over cool and dry.

POPULAR NAME: **Wart Plant**

*Haworthia greenii*
Wart Plant

245

SCIENTIFIC NAME: *Aloe ciliaris* **Haw.**
FAMILY: *Liliaceae*

Belonging to the Lily Family, the genus *Aloe* includes tree-like and climbing species, as well as dwarf, rosette-forming, leaf-succulent plants. Almost all possess beautiful blossoms. *Aloe ciliaris* inhabits the undergrowth of the forests and the bush of the Cape Province of South Africa. It grows over 5 metres (16 feet) long but only 1 to 1.5 cm (about $\frac{1}{2}$ inch) through and climbs high up into the trees. Their leaves grow 10 to 15 cm (4 to 6 inches) long. The inflorescence, 20 to 30 cm (8 to 12 inches) high, bears many individual blossoms 3 cm (1 inch) long.

CARE: The growing season of the Aloe as a rule falls in autumn and winter in the Northern Hemisphere. For this reason and during this period, it requires a relatively large amount of water. This is especially true if it is kept warm through the winter. If it winters over cooler, then it should be watered less. *Aloe ciliaris* blooms from January to March. In the summer rest period, Aloes need less moisture. In summer, they can be kept in a suitable place in the open. It is also possible to so cultivate the South African Aloe that its growing season falls in our summer.

POPULAR NAME: **Climbing Aloe**

*Aloe ciliaris*
Climbing Aloe

SCIENTIFIC NAME: *Aloe striata* **Haw.**
FAMILY: *Liliaceae*

The stemless, rosette-forming *Aloe striata* has almost toothless leaves, which grow 45 to 50 cm (18 to 20 inches) long and 10 to 15 cm (4 to 6 inches) wide. The leaves are very attractive with their blue-green color and white margins. The blossoms appear from April to May in the North Temperate Zone in 20 or more clusters on the inflorescence, which is 60 to 90 cm (24 to 35 inches) high. Unfortunately, this plant requires a good deal of room. Small species such as the Cape Province *Aloe aristata* Haw. are better suited for the flower window. Their leaf rosettes grow to a width of 15 cm (6 inches) at the most. The flower stem, though, grows 50 cm (20 inches) high.

POPULAR NAME: **Coral Aloe**

*Aloe striata*
Coral Aloe

SCIENTIFIC NAME: *Agave victoriae-reginae* T. Moore
FAMILY: *Liliaceae*

Most Agaves grow much too large for window or small greenhouse cultivation. All the more welcome, then, are small species such as the illustrated, exceptionally beautiful *Agave victoriae-reginae* from Mexico. The rosettes of this species, which has an abundance of forms, do not grow broader than 50 to 60 cm (20 to 24 inches); the leaves measure 5 to 6 cm (2 to $2\frac{1}{2}$ inches) wide, and 10 to 15 cm (4 to 6 inches) long. The inflorescence, though, grows to a height of up to 4 metres (13 feet), of which the cream-colored spike takes up 3 metres (10 feet). Since the plant dies after it has ceased blooming, it is propagated seasonally by means of seeds.

CARE: Agaves in summer like to be in a bright, airy—not drafty—and sunny location. They can be simply left in the open. During this time, they need a lot of water. In winter, keep them cool and quite dry. The temperatures for *Agave victoriae-reginae* should not fall below 10° C. (50° F.).

POPULAR NAME: **Queen Agave**

*Agave victoriae-reginae*
Queen Agave

# Scientific Name Index

**253**

# Popular Name Index